POWER EVANGELISM

Power Evangelism

John Wimber
with Kevin Springer

1817

Harper & Row, Publishers, San Francisco

Cambridge, Hagerstown, New York, Philadelphia
London, Mexico City, São Paulo, Singapore, Sydney

FIRST EDITION

Library of Congress Cataloging-in-Publication Data

Wimber, John.
  Power evangelism.

  Bibliography: p.
  1. Evangelistic work.   2. Spiritual healing.   3. Miracles.
I. Springer, Kevin.
BV3793.W53   1986   231.7′3   85-45728
ISBN 0-06-069532-3

---

86 87 88 89 90 RRD 10 9 8 7 6 5 4 3 2 1

Dedicated to my wife, Carol,
without whom none of these things
would have meaning

Contents

Foreword

Power Evangelism is a remarkable book, a tract for the times. Its appearance at this point in history could not be more propitious. In the providence of God, we who are alive today are participants in the most massive and dramatic ingathering into the Christian church that has ever taken place. The events of the book of Acts can be seen as a mere pilot project in comparison to the current spread of the gospel and growth of the church worldwide. In this book John Wimber provides clues to a powerful spiritual instrument which, when used with dedication and discernment, could advance the process of world evangelization by a quantum leap.

Evangelism accompanied by supernatural signs and wonders is as old as the New Testament. Contemporary research has confirmed that such "power evangelism" has accompanied the spread of the gospel, especially on the frontiers of the clash between Christianity and paganism, through the centuries. True, the degree and intensity of the role of the miraculous in missions and evangelism has experienced ebbs and flows throughout history. The latter part of the nineteenth century and the early part of the twentieth can be seen as a time of an ebb, especially for those of us who are in the mainstream of evangelical Christianity. We were strongly influenced by dispensationalism on the one hand and Princeton theologian Benjamin Breckenridge Warfield on the other to believe that supernatural healings and miracles as a part of the ongoing ministry of the church had ceased with the end of the apostolic age and the close of the canon of Scripture.

Pentecostals began to turn the ebb into a flow at the turn of the century. They practiced power evangelism, but they had not reached a critical mass and their growth was relatively slow over the first fifty years of the movement. They were joined in spirit by the charismatic movement at mid-century. The charismatic movement flourished both within denominational structures and in newly created independent churches and movements. By 1985 the rates of growth of Pentecostal and charismatic churches were by far outstripping the other churches in virtually every part of the world. Current estimates put the number of Pentecostal and charismatic Christians worldwide at 120 million. The Assemblies of God in Brazil alone now report 12 million members. The Full Gospel Central Church in Seoul, Korea, has gathered half a million members into one local congregation.

While most of this church growth was taking place, neither John Wimber nor I counted ourselves as participants. In 1975 I invited John to come to work for the Fuller Evangelistic Association, which I directed, to pioneer what is now known as the Charles E. Fuller Institute for Evangelism and Church Growth. In that position John soon gained national recognition as a church growth trainer and consultant. He also joined the Fuller Seminary faculty as an adjunct professor and assisted me in teaching classes in the Doctor of Ministry program. While neither one of us was closed to the idea, healing the sick was light-years away from our teaching and ministry.

Toward the end of 1977 God led John Wimber to turn the Fuller Institute over to the capable leadership of Carl George to begin a new church which would later be known as Vineyard Christian Fellowship of Anaheim. In this book you will read the fascinating story of how God led Wimber into a ministry of healing the sick and casting out demons. I was an interested spectator, discreetly keeping somewhat aloof. But my respect for John's integrity as a pastor and a Christian brother was never in question. And as a professor of church growth I could not help but be impressed with the growth of the Vineyard from a home Bible study of seventeen to over six thousand.

I became a participant when John Wimber began teaching a course at Fuller under my supervision. In January of 1982 an experimental course, carrying the catalog number MC:510, was instituted. In the optional ministry session following one of the lectures, John prayed for the alleviation of a high-blood-pressure condition I had, and I was healed. That was only one of a succession of events that has brought me personally into a ministry of praying for the sick and seeing the power of God in operation. Among other things, I have come into an intimacy with Jesus that I had not known in the preceding twenty-five or thirty years of my ministry.

I say all that to say this: reading this book will help bring you to a place where God can use you to minister powerfully to others. If you are a Pentecostal or charismatic, the book will deepen your faith and in many cases bring you back to your roots. If you are not (as I am not), you will find that power evangelism can be compatible with the mainstream Christian life-style. John Wimber has a special anointing to address a wide spectrum of the body of Christ and communicate to them that Jesus Christ is the same yesterday, today, and forever.

As you read, especially if some of this material is new to you, do so with an open mind and an open heart. John Wimber has a message that we all need to hear and then to act upon. If we do so, we will see the remarkable harvest now being gathered in the name of Jesus increased manifold. The gospel will spread "with signs following," millions of names will be entered in the Lamb's Book of Life, the angels of heaven will be greatly rejoicing, and, most important of all, God's name will be glorified.

C. Peter Wagner
Fuller Seminary School of World Mission
Pasadena, California

Acknowledgments

There are many people whose support through prayer and suggestions aided the writing of this book. First, I would like to thank my mentor, partner, and friend, C. Peter Wagner, who introduced me not only to church growth but also to the church around the world. Without his encouragement and insights, I could not have written this book. I am also thankful for the late George Ladd, whose pioneering work on the kingdom of God forms the theological foundation for power evangelism.

The faculty of the School of World Mission at Fuller Theological Seminary in Pasadena, California, sponsored and encouraged MC:510, ''The Miraculous and Church Growth,'' a course in which much of the material in this book was developed.

Russell P. Spittler, professor of New Testament at Fuller Seminary, gave many hours in reading and commenting on an early draft, providing helpful suggestions that improved the book.

Most of all I thank Jesus for so graciously working in my life, showing me more of his kingdom and compassion, despite my many shortcomings and failures. To him be all glory, blessing, and praise.

John Wimber

During the past year I have had the privilege of coming to know John Wimber not only as an author but as a friend. In that time I have seen that he lives what he teaches. I thank him for entrusting me with the task of writing and editing material that God has built into his life.

No writer is any better than his or her editors. In my case, I must begin with the man who taught me most of what I know about writing. Kevin Perrotta, managing editor of *Pastoral Renewal*, gave many hours in reading, commenting, and editing the early drafts. His corrections and suggestions improved the book immensely.

My wife, Suzanne, patiently read every computer printout of each chapter, never complaining about the continual changes associated with the writing of any book. She is my greatest colleague, best critic, and eternal friend.

Finally, I would like to thank my pastor, Ray Nethery, who for sixteen years has encouraged and supported me in all that God has called me to do. His example of Christian maturity has always challenged me to aspire for excellence and integrity in all that I do.

Kevin Springer

Introduction

I knew little about God when I converted to Christianity in 1962. A fourth-generation unbeliever, I had received no Christian training as a child. As an adult I had neither belonged to nor regularly attended a church. At twenty-nine years of age, I was a jazz musician with a soaring career and a diving marriage. The reason for my conversion to Christianity was simple: my life was in shambles and I was told a personal relationship with Jesus Christ offered hope from the despair. Certainly my conversion was not the result of sincere intellectual inquiry into the mysteries of God.

Carol, my wife, also committed her life to Christ in 1962. A young mother with three children and another on the way, she had to contend with my disorderly life-style and her own gnawing sense of guilt for having turned away from her Christian heritage. She had been raised in the church and had attended Christian parochial schools. So, like me, she too turned to Christianity out of deep personal need, but, unlike mine, her conversion also had an intellectual component. Her questions—about God and Satan, heaven and hell, salvation and damnation—were many and urgent. For Carol, reasonable answers to these questions were the foundation of faith.

For both of us the results of our conversions were the same: freedom from guilt and the fear of death, a purpose for living, and a renewed marriage. We also immediately plunged into personal evangelism. There were so many who had not heard the gospel! Family members, friends, strangers—anyone willing to listen—heard the news of Jesus from us. But soon it became apparent that Carol and I each approached evangelism differently, perhaps accounted for by our dissimilar backgrounds.

For Carol, a clear, logical presentation of the gospel was central to the evangelistic task. She wanted to answer all the questions (even when people were not asking them!), always aiming for a solid intellectual base to the conversion. I relied more on my intuition, a spiritual guidance system that told me when people were ready to give their lives to Christ. Frequently I interrupted Carol's presentations (much to her consternation) and asked the person we were talking with if he or she wanted to receive Jesus Christ at that very moment. Inevitably the person wanted to pray. Unlike Carol's, my basic assumption was that even with only minimal information about Christ, one may begin a personal relationship with him. Evangelism, I thought, did not necessitate passing on a great deal of information about Christ. But I was uneasy about how much knowledge was necessary for faith in Christ, and why some people needed so little while others needed more.

C. S. Lewis's conversion captures the interplay—and mystery—of faith and reason in the conversion process. Raised in the Anglican Church of Ireland, Lewis had no more than a nominal belief. By the time he was confirmed at age sixteen he considered himself an atheist, only attending church to please his father. As a schoolboy he was tutored by the renowned dialectician W. T. Kirkpatrick. Kirkpatrick was a professed atheist who trained Lewis to "talk to victory" and always insisted on precision of terms and clarity of logic in his arguments.

After serving in the army during World War I and completing his education at Oxford, Lewis was elected to a fellowship in English Language and Literature at Magdalen College, Oxford, a position he held for the next thirty years. It was at Oxford that Lewis came into contact with Christian intellectuals like Neville Coghill, J. R. R. Tolkien, and Owen Barfield. Later they, along with the novelist Charles Williams, would form the core of the "Inklings," a group of Oxford dons who met weekly to read their writings aloud and discuss them. Through the quiet witness of the future Inklings and the influence of his own readings ("A young man who wishes to remain a sound atheist cannot be too careful of his reading," he later wrote), Lewis slowly inched toward Christianity.

In 1929, at age thirty-two, he was converted to belief in a personal God. Later he wrote, "Amiable agnostics will talk cheerfully about 'man's search for God.' To me, as I was then, they might as well have talked about a mouse's search for the cat."

Even though he believed in God, for some time Lewis struggled with the claims of Jesus and the gospel. It was two years later, while he was riding to a local zoo in the sidecar of his brother Warren's motorcycle, that his conversion to Christ was completed. It was not a dramatic sort of conversion: all he could say later was, "When we set out I did not believe that Jesus Christ is the Son of God, and when we reached the zoo I did."

I have described C. S. Lewis's conversion to drive home a point: after all the years of doubting and seeking, debate and reading, for no apparent reason, in the sidecar of a motorcycle, he believed in Christ. His search had been important, but in the end it took no more than a motorcycle ride with his brother to complete his conversion. His time of faith had come.

As a pastor in the late sixties and early seventies, I continued to feel a tension between the intellectual and intuitive aspects of the evangelistic task. Then, in 1974, shortly after joining the staff of the Charles E. Fuller Institute of Evangelism and Church Growth in Pasadena, California, I learned about the "Engel Scale," a model that describes the various stages in thinking (from little knowledge to a lot) and attitudes (from hostile to responsive) that people frequently go through in conversion (see Chapter 4). This was a hallmark for me, because James F. Engel's research demonstrated that in most societies there is always a group of people who are on the verge of converting to Christianity, and their openness to it involves both intellectual and attitudinal factors. Further, Dr. Engel asserted that the most effective type of evangelism aims at this group. C. S. Lewis, when he went on his motorcycle trip to the zoo, was on the verge, ready for harvesting. As a young Christian I had a knack for identifying members of that open group and leading them to Christian commitment. The Engel Scale helped me understand who these people were and why aiming only at their intellects was not the most effective way to evangelize them.

So Carol and I were both right. For effective evangelism there must be the message, the content of the gospel: "Faith comes from hearing the message, and the message is heard through the word of Christ" (Rom. 10:17). And there also must be right timing—the person must be ready, ripened for harvest. Among most western evangelicals, the intellectual task frequently is stressed to the exclusion of the intuitive.

Also around this time I was introduced to C. Peter Wagner's writings on the goals of personal evangelism (see Chapter 3). Dr. Wagner points out that too often Western evangelicals' goal is merely to help people make a *decision* to follow Christ, whereas the great commission passage in Matthew 28:19–20 calls for the making of full disciples: Christians who not only believe but are trained and living out the demands of the gospel. This confirmed my suspicion that many evangelicals place a priority on the intellectual aspects of the gospel that often results in a confusion of intellectual ascent (knowing *about* Christ) with faith itself, and of right thinking with right living.

This is not to belittle the importance of the Christian mind and good theology. A central task of evangelism is the bold proclamation of the gospel, a clear and precise presentation of the death, burial, and resurrection of Christ. But for this message to be heard and understood there must be more than the dissemination of information. Dr. Wagner calls the making of disciples the result of persuasion evangelism. Well into the seventies I was still confused about how consistently to practice persuasion evangelism, evangelism that produces not just decisions but disciples of Christ. There had to be another element, a missing part, that would catalyze personal evangelism.

Then I was introduced to another of Dr. Wagner's books, *Look Out! The Pentecostals Are Coming*. I had always avoided Pentecostal and charismatic Christians, in part because it seemed that often controversy and division surrounded their ministries. Also, my judgment of their ministries was colored by a presupposition that charismatic gifts like tongues, prophecy, and healing were not for today. (As a dispensationalist, I believed the charismatic gifts ceased at the end of the first century.) But in Dr. Wagner I encountered a credible witness, an accomplished missionary and dean of Fuller Theological Seminary's School of World Mission, who wrote that healing and deliverance from evil spirits were happening in South America today. Further, he proved that these miraculous encounters resulted in large evangelistic harvests and church growth. His book forced me to reconsider my position on the charismatic gifts, though I was still skeptical of their validity today.

With this new openness, I read books by Donald Gee (an English Pentecostal who wrote *Concerning Spiritual Gifts*) and Morton Kelsey (*Healing and Christianity*) on the charismatic gifts. Their writings, combined with first-person testimonies of the miraculous from Third World students at Fuller Theological Seminary's School of World Mission, opened me to a new understanding of the part the Holy Spirit plays in evangelism. While I did not agree with all that Gee and Kelsey wrote (and still do not), I had to reconsider much that I had been taught about the charismatic gifts.

I also reevaluated my experiences in personal evangelism. Slowly I began to realize that my ability to know people's concerns and when they were ready to convert to Christ—what previously I thought were merely psychological insights—possibly were spiritual gifts like a word of knowledge or a word of wisdom. I wondered, had I for years been experiencing these spiritual gifts in my evangelistic efforts?

As I searched the Gospels to learn more about the gifts I discovered another significant point: Jesus always combined the proclamation of the kingdom of God with its demonstration (the casting out of demons, healing the sick, raising the dead, and so on). The spiritual gifts took on new meaning for me. Scripture indicated that they authenticated the gospel, cutting through people's resistance and drawing attention to the good news of Jesus Christ. No wonder Jesus was so effective in evangelism.

By 1977 my thinking regarding personal evangelism was significantly altered. Once I accepted the fact that all the spiritual gifts are for today, I found a key for effective evangelism: combining the proclamation with the demonstration of gospel. (In fact, it is accurate to say that my search for more effective evangelism led in part to the spiritual gifts.) Rather than detracting from the proclamation of the gospel, the gifts, I observed, when correctly practiced, open people to a clearer understanding and practice of Christianity. There is unusual power and effectiveness in this form of evangelism, which is the reason that I call it "power evangelism."

While my understanding and practice of evangelism, the Holy Spirit, and church growth were undergoing a revolution, I still lacked a biblical theology that integrated the three, a grid for understanding how they are supposed to work together and fulfill God's purpose on earth. This last element—a solid, evangelical theology—is the foundation on which all practice must stand. I was already acquainted with George Eldon Ladd's writings (he was a Fuller Theological Seminary professor), but it was not until I read his book *Jesus and the Kingdom* that I realized how his work on the kingdom of God formed a theological basis for power evangelism. As I read Dr. Ladd's works, and then read afresh the Gospel accounts, I became convinced that power evangelism was for today.

I do not believe that it is enough for Christians to gather information, understand new facts—even think differently about the supernatural in Scripture—if it does not affect how we live. At the core of my being I am an activist. Regarding power evangelism, this meant that I needed to field-test my newfound theology, to go out into the world and see if what I thought Scripture taught in fact worked in Western society. So in 1978 I left the Charles E. Fuller Institute of Evangelism and Church Growth to become pastor of what is now called the Vineyard Christian Fellowship of Anaheim, California. It was in this environment, a small group of fifty people, that I first tested my theories of power evangelism. Today that small group has grown into a movement of forty thousand people in a hundred and forty congregations around the United States and Canada. Many of the experiences described on the following pages are drawn from these congregations.

Because a theology of the kingdom of God is the biblical and theological foundation for power evangelism, I begin the book appropriately with a chapter explaining Jesus' teaching on the kingdom. The next six chapters, the heart of the book, explain and illustrate power evangelism today and throughout church history. In my research I discovered that there is nothing new or novel about power evangelism.

In the final chapters I address the implications of power evangelism for conservative evangelicalism, Pentecostalism, and the charismatic renewal in mainline denominations and the Roman Catholic church. Though I write about power evangelism, the most powerful evangelism will come only when Jesus' prayer for Christian unity is fulfilled: "May they be brought to complete unity to let the world know that you sent me and have loved them even as you have loved me" (John 17:23). I pray that what I write about power evangelism will contribute to that unity.

1. The Kingdom of God

The good news Jesus proclaimed was the gospel of the kingdom of God. "The time has come," Mark summarizes Jesus as preaching at the beginning of his public ministry. "The kingdom of God is near. Repent and believe the good news!" (Mark 1:15). Thus the heart of Jesus' message was both the proclamation of God's action—"The kingdom is near"—and the demand for a response from all who heard—"Repent and believe."

Jesus was saying to his Jewish audience that his Father's promise to their father, Abraham, was about to be fulfilled:

I will make you into a great nation
    and I will bless you;
I will make your name great,
    and you will be a blessing.
I will bless those who bless you,
    and whoever curses you I will curse;
and all peoples on earth
    will be blessed through you (Gen. 12:2–3).

Jesus was proclaiming nothing less than the hope of Israel's salvation, that God was coming to redeem and bless them and establish his reign over all the earth. This salvation was summed up in the idea that "the kingdom of God" was close. For the duration of his public ministry, Jesus demonstrated that the kingdom of God was near by healing the sick, casting out demons, and raising the dead. Every miraculous act had a purpose: to confront people with his message that the kingdom had come and that they had to decide to accept or reject it.

Despite different ideas about what the hope of salvation would look like (there were in Christ's day many interpretations), all Jews eagerly anticipated a day of salvation, a time of fulfillment. But what did the "kingdom of God" mean to Jesus and his listeners? From where did the term come? Through the parables and their interpretations (usually given privately to the disciples), Christ transformed what was commonly accepted about the kingdom of God in his day. To understand what most first-century Jews assumed about their hope for salvation, we must begin by looking at the kingdom of God in the Old Testament.

A POLITICAL KINGDOM

For most of their history, the Jews lived under the domination of foreign nations and foreign kings. After the wilderness wanderings and the conquest of Canaan, the Israelites achieved their only real period of national independence and unity under King David. Upon his son Solomon's death, the nation divided into the northern kingdom of Israel and the southern kingdom of Judah. The next two hundred years saw civil war, threats from foreign kings, and a series of rulers on the throne of each kingdom. During this period the Jews longed for a time in the future when God would restore the Davidic blessings of the past.

At this time the concept of the Day of the Lord arose. The prophets coined this phrase, by which people understood a time when God would restore his people, Israel, as a unified political and geographical entity. Salvation meant the return of a single, strong Jewish nation, as in the days of King David (see Isa. 11). But the prophets proclaimed that this was a two-sided coin and the flip side of salvation was judgment—judgment of the nations and even Israel (see Amos 1).

After the fall of the Northern Kingdom to the Assyrians in 721 B.C. and the conquest of the Southern Kingdom and subsequent exile of the Jews to Babylon in 587 B.C., hope promised by the coming of the Day of the Lord was ever more desired (Ps. 126). When the Persian emperor Cyrus allowed the exiled Jews to return to Jerusalem in 538 B.C. and rebuild the Temple under Zerubbabel, a descendant of David, people thought the kingdom would be established. But their aspirations were not realized. Israel remained governed and controlled by foreign nations—the Persians, the Greeks, and finally the Romans in Christ's time. Still, the Jews never stopped looking for the Anointed One—the Messiah—who would lead them to renewed political glory.

This appears to be what the Jews in general were looking for at the time of Christ and how they understood him when he spoke of the kingdom. John 6:15 clearly supports this. The people wanted to make Jesus king of Israel by force. Even the disciples, after being with him for years, longed for the restoration of Israel (Acts 1:6).

In summary, the prophets presented the kingdom of God— what they called the Day of the Lord—as a kingdom of this world, peopled by Jews. It was not a spiritual and otherworldly kingdom; it was the dream of Jewish nationalism.[1]

CAUGHT BETWEEN TWO AGES

But this was not the only popularly accepted understanding of the kingdom of God in Christ's days. During the intertestamental period (approximately 200 B.C. to the New Testament era), the time in which the apocalyptic literature[2] was written, the term "kingdom of God" came into widespread usage. As was true for the Day of the Lord, hope was prominent, but it assumed a new meaning. The hope of the prophets was for a historical, political kingdom, but the apocalyptic writers saw an end coming to the present age, after which God would create a new world in which all evil, demons, sickness, and death would be defeated.[3]

This "present age" was thought to be dominated by Satan, an idea that came out of the frightful persecutions unleashed

by Antiochus Epiphanes, the king of Syria from 175 to 164
B.C. who tried to Hellenize the Jews, inciting the revolt of the
Maccabees. The Jews believed that such hell on earth was the
result of cosmic turmoil.

In the pseudepigraphal book of Jubilees (chap. 23) the age
to come (the Golden Age) is ushered in by God himself.[4] It
reverses the evils of Satan, who appears as the ruler of a
counterkingdom of evil. Good triumphs. Healing and the expulsion of demons abound.

THE KINGDOM IN THE NEW TESTAMENT

Jesus in part held these views. He uses Old Testament and
intertestamental terms like the "kingdom of God" and "ages,"
building on their popularly accepted meanings, to explain why
he came. For example, in explaining the parable of the wheat
and the weeds, Jesus uses terms like the "sons of the kingdom," "sons of the evil one," "the end of the age," and "the
righteous will shine like the sun in the kingdom of their Father"
(Matt. 13:36–43; see also 1 Cor. 2:6; Gal. 1:4). He taught the
disciples that like the Old Testament prophets he too saw a
day of judgment soon coming for the nations, the Son of Man
being the Judge. And like the apocalyptic writers, he too fore-
saw a swift end coming to the present age and its replacement
by a future age—"the kingdom of [the] Father."

George Ladd summarizes scriptural teaching on the ages
with these words:

In brief, this age, which extends from creation to the Day of the
Lord . . . is the age of human existence in weakness and mortality,
of evil, sin, and death. The age to come will see the realization of all
that the reign of God means, and will be the age of resurrection into
eternal life in the kingdom of God. Everything in the Gospels points
to the idea that life in the kingdom of God in the age to come will be
life on the earth—but life transformed by the kingly rule of God
when his people enter into the full measure of the divine blessings
(Matt. 19:28).[5]

The following diagram, adapted from the work of George Ladd, helps visualize the present and future aspects of the kingdom of God:[6]

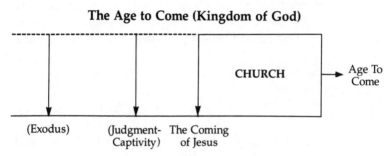

The Age to Come (Kingdom of God)

CHURCH   → Age To Come

(Exodus)   (Judgment-   The Coming
            Captivity)   of Jesus

This Present Evil Age

It was with this understanding that John the Baptist made his announcement: "Repent, for the kingdom of heaven is near" (Matt. 3:2). God was ready to bring the new age into existence. John announced the new age would soon be here. Jesus said, "The kingdom of God has come upon you" (Matt. 12:28).

In the New Testament, the Greek word *basileia* means "kingship" or "royal rule." It is normally translated "kingdom." It implies exercise of kingly rule or reign rather than simply a geographic realm over which a king rules. Westerners conceive of kingdoms largely in terms of realms. For example, the United Kingdom conjures thoughts of the territory encompassing British lands. The biblical concept goes beyond the idea of a realm to emphasize rule.

This is what Jesus meant when he said that the kingdom or rulership of God had come *in him*. The authority of God had come to claim what was rightfully his. The future age, the kingdom of God, invaded the present age, the kingdom of Satan.[7] To use an expression of George Ladd's, we live in "the presence of the future." We are between the times, as it were, between the inauguration and the consummation of the kingdom of God.

This explains the twofold pattern of Christ's ministry, repeated wherever he went: first *proclamation*, then *demonstration*. First he preached repentance and the good news of the kingdom of God. Then he cast out demons, healed the sick, raised the dead—which proved he was the presence of the kingdom, the Anointed One.

Jesus came as a Jew to Israel. He accepted the authority of the Old Testament and basically ministered to the "lost sheep of Israel" (Matt. 10:5–7). Kingdom rule was first offered to the Jews, but Israel rejected Christ and his kingdom. Jesus was disappointed (Matt. 23:37–39). While Israel *as a nation* rejected Christ, a remnant did accept him, and these few were the foundation of the New Testament church (Rom. 11:1–24). Jesus called twelve disciples, symbolizing the continuity between the disciples and the twelve tribes of Israel (Matt. 19:28). By choosing the Twelve Jesus taught that he was raising up a new people to replace the nation that was rejecting his message.

Christ's blessing of Peter and his giving him the "keys of the kingdom of heaven" (Matt. 16:18–19) is best understood in terms of the Old Testament idea of Israel as the people of God.[8] His announcement to Peter, "You are Peter, and on this rock I will build my church," was in perfect continuity with Old Testament Israel's concept of building a nation. Jesus was using Old Testament images, especially those taken from the prophets (Jer. 1:10; Amos 9:11–12). In the New Testament, the church enters into the covenant blessings of Israel.[9]

When Israel rejected the kingdom of God, Christ handed his rule, the place of redemption and focus of his works, over to the church (Matt. 21:33–46). Therefore, the church has the "keys"—the way—to the kingdom. Jesus took the keys away from the Pharisees, because they had taken away the key of knowledge of the kingdom from the people (Luke 11:45–52). As George Ladd would say, the keys are spiritual insights and authority that enabled Peter to lead others through the door of revelation. The keys are to the narrow path to the kingdom of God.[10]

The authority to bind or loose involves admission or exclusion of men and women from the kingdom of God.[11] The proclamation and demonstration of the kingdom of Christ provide the opportunity for people to enter eternal life (Matt. 10:14, 15, 40).

Kingdoms have three elements: a king, authority, and subjects. If one of these is missing, we do not have a kingdom. Jesus is our King; all authority in heaven and earth has been given him by his Father; Christians are his subjects.

Some Christians, unclear about the relationship between the kingdom of God and the church, confuse the two and teach that the church *is* the kingdom. This leads to serious error, such as equating membership in the church with final salvation. The church is an avenue to salvation, in so far as it leads people to union with Christ, but the church is not the source of salvation.

The kingdom of God created the church at Pentecost through the outpouring of the Holy Spirit. The church is the primary (though not exclusive) residence of God's rule. This means the church witnesses to the kingdom, but it does not have authority in itself to build the kingdom; only God has that authority. When the church is confused with the kingdom, leaders assume God's authority resides in their office, that they are the rule of God. Authoritarianism and even cultishness can be an unfortunate result of this kind of thinking. When pastoral leaders understand that their authority is derived from the kingdom of God and that rule is not equated with office, they are restrained from leading in their own authority.

The church is also the instrument of the kingdom. The disciples not only proclaimed the kingdom, they demonstrated the works and miracles of the kingdom. Jesus told Peter that the "gates of Hades will not overcome [the church]" (Matt. 16:18). The "gates of Hades" are the strongholds of evil and death, satanic powers that seek to destroy us (Eph. 6:10–12).[12]

As Christ's instruments, we war on these strongholds, replacing their dominion with the kingdom of God.

With this in mind Christ commissioned the Twelve (Matt. 10:5–15), the Seventy-two (Luke 10:1–20), and now commissions us (Matt. 28:18–20). During the forty days between his resurrection and ascension, Jesus spoke to the apostles about the kingdom of God (Acts 1:3). In Samaria, Philip "preached the good news of the kingdom of God" (Acts 8:12), and Peter, James, and Paul all mention the kingdom of God in their Letters.[13]

THE GOSPEL OF THE KINGDOM

Proclamation of a faulty gospel will produce faulty or, at best, weak Christians. Such is the case all too often today. Instead of a call to the lordship of Christ and membership in his kingdom, people are hearing a gospel that emphasizes self: come to Jesus and get this or that need met, be personally fulfilled, reach your potential. This, however, is not the costly kingdom gospel that Christ proclaims: "Whoever wants to save his life will lose it, but whoever loses his life for me and for the gospel will save it" (Mark 8:35).

Often the kingdom is likened to a Caribbean cruise on a luxury liner. People change into their leisure clothes, grab their suntan lotion, and saunter down to the docks. What a shock it is when they find that entering the kingdom is really more like enlisting in the navy and doing battle with the enemy.

BATTLEFRONTS

The enemy follows no rules of war. Satan considers nothing unfair; he is not a gentleman. The sooner Christians understand this, the more serious they will become about being equipped and properly trained for the kingdom.

Although he follows no rules, we know Satan attacks on

three fronts: through the flesh, through the world, and by direct assault. Because this book is primarily concerned with the assaults of Satan, I will only make a few comments on the first two, devoting the remainder of the chapter to the latter.[14]

The flesh: In the 1936 Spanish civil war, Franco's Loyalist Army defeated the Republican Army in Madrid. It was the key battle of the war and led to the establishment of Franco's government in Spain. When asked what the key to his victory was, Franco replied, "the fifth column." He had four columns of troops engaged openly and a "fifth column" of loyalists *inside* Madrid who, through sabotage, seriously weakened the Republican Army.

We too have a fifth column, "sinful passions" that reside in our members. In Paul's words, "I know that nothing good lives in me, that is, in my sinful nature" (Rom. 7:18). The enemy loves to exploit our fifth column through temptation, but God has given us the power to walk by faith and resist that temptation.

The world: Psalm 137 says, "How can we sing the songs of the Lord while in a foreign land?" How can Christians serve God's kingdom while taking on the values and life-styles of the world? We cannot.

When we think of ourselves as an army, the issue of discipline and fulfillment of kingdom standards becomes more critical than personal security and ease. Sometimes a soldier looks at civilian life and says, "That life-style looks attractive. I like the glitter of materialism, the thrill of personal power, the pleasure of sexual immorality, the quest for self-fulfillment. That life sure beats this one." When that happens, discipline is lost, and we are infiltrated and eventually taken captive. Paul has strong advice about this: "No one serving as a soldier gets involved in civilian affairs—he wants to please his commanding officer" (2 Tim. 2:4).

We have been given the keys to the kingdom, the authority and power over the enemy, but if we do not exercise that power, it is of no use. The kingdom of darkness is organized to distract us, to prevent us from doing God's bidding. Through the glitter of materialism and power, sexual immorality, and the promise of self-fulfillment, Satan diverts our attention from the kingdom of God.

Fellowship with other Christians in local churches—outposts of the kingdom—is a primary defense against being taken in by the world. Prayer, Scripture study, and spiritual disciplines like fasting are necessary not only to gain God's power and insight but also to equip us to resist the world.

The devil: In John 10:10 we read that Satan has well-defined objectives: "The thief comes only to steal and kill and destroy." We also observe that it is the devil and his demons, not men and women, against whom we war (Eph. 6:12).

Our situation is similar to an underground army living in a land still occupied by a defeated enemy. Such was the French underground's role after D-Day during World War II. The Germans were still capable of committing atrocities on French civilians even though the Germans' eventual defeat was sure. The 1984 arrest and trial of Claus Barbie illustrates how barbarous the Germans' acts were: knowing there was no hope for Germany victory, Barbie nevertheless tortured and murdered hundreds of French—including children. He was nicknamed "the Butcher of Lyon."

Satan has many names too: Destroyer, Deceiver, Liar—the Butcher of the World. In our war with Satan, there are no demilitarized zones. There is never a lull in the fighting. We are born into the fight, and—unless the Day of the Lord comes—we will die in the fight. We should never expect the battle to cease.

The kingdom of Satan was and is Christ's real enemy, and there is a war on. Jesus is about his Father's business, which is releasing those held captive by Satan. The final outcome of the battle has been assured through Christ's death, resurrection, and ascension to the place of all authority, the right hand of the Father (1 Cor. 15:20–28). But Satan is not yet cast out and will not be until Christ returns to establish his kingdom

forever. So we are caught between two ages. The fight continues and we are in it.

POWER AND AUTHORITY

To fight effectively, we must correctly understand power and
authority in the kingdom. In Luke 9:1–2 we read: "When Jesus
had called the Twelve together, *he gave them power and authority*
to drive out all demons and to cure diseases, and he sent them
out to preach the kingdom of God and to heal the sick." He
gave them power and authority to cure diseases and drive out
all demons. Everyone, according to Acts 1:8, can receive power
from the Holy Spirit. Power is the ability, the strength, the
might to complete a given task. Authority is the right to use
the power of God.

For example, a traffic policeman does not have the physical
power to stop cars. However, he does stop them, because he
wears a badge and uniform given him by a higher authority.
We have been given a badge and uniform by Jesus. These gifts
become effective when we learn to wear and use them correctly.

In Scripture, the centurion understood how authority and
power work (see Matt. 8:5–13). He was a man both under the
authority of some and having authority over others. He knew
how to receive and give orders. After asking Jesus to heal his
paralyzed servant—to which Jesus responded he would "go
and heal him"—the centurion replied: "Just say the word, and
my servant will be healed." Jesus, "astonished" by the centurion's words, said, "I have not found anyone in Israel with
such great faith."

Our difficulty is that we have not learned to receive or give
orders. To a great extent, we practice a cosmetic Christianity,
because we misunderstand our initial call to Christ. We think
that the key for maturity and power is to be "good." We then
focus on our behavior, but our behavior never meets the high
standards of Christ's righteousness.

I did this for years. By focusing on my behavior, I was in constant turmoil, because my behavior was never good enough, never meeting God's standards (or my standards) of righteousness. I first believed in Christ because I was not good, yet after becoming a Christian I still struggled in my own strength with not being good enough. So I was always under conviction, always struggling with guilt.

Then one day, sixteen years ago, I fell to my knees and asked God to help me. He responded, "Since you can do nothing without me, how much help do you want?" Then he said, "The issue is not being good, it is being God's. Just come to me, and I'll provide goodness for you."

I did not fully understand his words. What did he mean, "I'll provide goodness for you"? I was confused, so for the next five years I tried to be good in my own strength. I soon became more and more despondent. Finally, I began to ask God about what he had told me earlier concerning his goodness. He explained that he had good works prepared for me, but they were *his* works, and *I* could not do them for him. He told me that I needed to begin to listen to his voice rather than try to distill the Christian life down to a set of rules and principles. I began to listen more during my times of prayer and Scripture study and more consciously talked with him throughout the normal activities of the day.

Then something interesting began to happen. He put new desires and attitudes in me. His Spirit began to strengthen me to do righteous acts I previously had no desire for. I began to hear his voice throughout the day. And good works were multiplied in my life.

Today I no longer try to be good; instead I am only concerned with doing God's bidding: what he commands, I do. Now my personal life is more conformed to his righteousness and character than it used to be. Following his commands does not leave much time for sin.

Most of us are confused about how to live a life of faith. We cannot understand or relate to the superhuman efforts it took to do the things that Jesus did. The reason is that too often we are searching for methods, formulas, and principles that will open the power of God to us, becoming frustrated each time we try another "key" that does not work.

Again, we are not the kingdom; we are instruments of the kingdom. The works of the kingdom are performed through us; thus our purpose is to witness about what God has done, is doing, and will do. Like Jesus, we have come to do the will of the Father. When asked how we should pray, Jesus taught us, "Our Father in heaven . . . your kingdom come, your will be done on earth as it is in heaven." As the centurion did, we must learn how to hear and believe Jesus' commands if we expect to be the vehicles of signs and miracles for the kingdom.

COSMIC WARFARE

James Kallas in *The Real Satan* says:

A war is going on! Cosmic war! Jesus is the divine invader sent by God to shatter the strengths of Satan. In that light, the whole ministry of Jesus unrolls. Jesus has one purpose—to defeat Satan. He takes seriously the strength of the enemy.[15]

Kallas's remarks raise a significant question: who is attacking the territory of the other, Christ or Satan, and what difference does the answer to this question make to Christians? The difference affects our attitude and stance toward the Christian life. If Jesus is the invader, Satan is consigned to the defensive. We become offensive soldiers, taking territory and redeeming lives—we are Christ's cobelligerents.

Jesus says the same thing in Matthew 11:12: "From the days of John the Baptist until now, the kingdom of heaven has been forcefully advancing, and forceful men lay hold of it." George Ladd points out that this verse may be interpreted several ways, depending on how the Greek term for "forcefully advancing" is translated. It may be understood as "to exercise force" or as "to be treated forcibly." The latter translation implies Satan wars directly on the kingdom of God, putting Christ and us on the defensive.

But Ladd argues that "we do not discover [in the New Testament] the idea of Satan attacking the kingdom of God or exercising his power against the kingdom itself. *He can only wage his war against the sons of the kingdom. . . . God is the aggressor; Satan is on the defensive*" (emphasis mine).[16] Ladd concludes that the best option is "the kingdom of heaven 'exercises its force' or 'makes its way powerfully' in the world."[17] We are thrust into the middle of a battle with Satan: it's a tug-of-war and the prize is the souls of men and women. Satan's captivity of men and women has many facets, but denying them final salvation is his primary goal. But there are other types of dominion: bondage to sin, physical and emotional problems, social disruption, and demonic affliction.

Our mission is to rescue those who have been taken captive as a result of Adam's fall. How we fulfill our mission is what the remainder of this book is about.

2. The Power Encounter

I was awakened late one night in 1978 by a desperate phone call. "Please, Pastor Wimber, come and help Melinda!" a young man cried into the telephone. He went on to explain that his friend Melinda (not her real name) was in a pick-up truck in a nearby field. Although she was only eighteen years old and weighed only a hundred pounds, she was thrashing about so violently that the truck was rocking. Strange growling, animal-like sounds were coming from her—not her normal voice at all.

I was to meet a demon.

Before this I had belived in the existence of demons and probably even met a few without knowing it, but this was the first time I met one who was openly manifesting all of its evil, lying, and foul deeds through another human being. This was a pastoral call that I would never forget.

After I arrived at the gas station, the boy took me to the truck. The girl, or rather something in the girl, spoke. "I know you" were the first words to assault me—packaged in a hoarse, eerie voice—"and you don't know what you're doing."

I thought, "You're right."

The demon then said through Melinda, "You can't do anything with her. She's mine."

I thought, "You're wrong."

Then began ten hours of spiritual warfare in which I called on the forces of heaven to overcome Satan. During this time I smelled putrid odors and saw her eyes roll back and her profuse perspiration. I heard blasphemy and saw wild physical activity that required more strength than a petite girl operating under her own power could possibly possess. I was appalled and very afraid, but I refused to give up the fight.

In the end I think the demon left because I wore it out, certainly not because I was skilled at casting out evil spirits. (Since that time I have learned much about this type of encounter. If I had known then what I know now, I am convinced the episode would not have taken longer than an hour.)[1]

THE BATTLE OF THE KINGDOMS

Encounters with demons have become a common experience for me. Missionary Alan Tippett calls these events *power encounters*, the clashing of the kingdom of God with the kingdom of Satan.[2] These conflicts, these clashes, may occur anywhere, anytime. The expulsion of demons is most dramatic, though power encounters are far from limited only to those where Satan takes the form of the demonic.

Any system or force that must be overcome for the gospel to be believed is cause for a power encounter. In each case, unbelief is the evil that is conquered in a power encounter. In fact, unbelief *is* the kingdom of Satan, albeit a far less visible form of him than demons or illness. When we experience the Spirit and are able to convert unbelievers, we are the vehicles through which the kingdom of God defeats the kingdom of Satan. This is especially true in the area of missions. Missiologist C. Peter Wagner, professor of church growth at Fuller Theological Seminary in Pasadena, California, commenting on power encounters and evangelism among tribal groups, writes that "a power encounter is a visible, practical demonstration that Jesus Christ is more powerful than the false gods or spirits worshiped or feared by a people group."[3] This results in the conversion of members of the tribal groups.

Jesus began his public ministry with a power encounter. Soon after his forty days of fasting and testing in the wilderness, he went throughout Galilee proclaiming the gospel and calling the first disciples. Eventually he arrived in Capernaum, where he attended a synagogue meeting. As was the tradition for visiting rabbis, Jesus taught the people. The people were "amazed at his teaching, because he taught them as one who had authority, not as the teachers of the law" (Mark 1:22). A demon-possessed man cried out, "What do you want with us, Jesus of Nazareth? Have you come to destroy us? I know who you are—the Holy One of God!"

Here was a clear challenge to the kingdom of God. How did Christ respond? He silenced the spirit, then called it out of the man. The people were impressed with his power: "He even gives orders to evil spirits and they obey him." That evening, in response to the morning's deliverance, a large crowd gathered near the place where he was staying, and he again drove out demons and "healed many who had various diseases" (Mark 1:34).

Probably the most dramatic illustration of this type of encounter in the Old Testament is found in the story of Elijah on Mount Carmel confronting the four hundred and fifty prophets of Baal (1 Kings 18). Here we see God's prophet encountering an impotent god, a graven image representing a religious system that Satan backed.

After the wicked King Ahab accused Elijah of causing trouble in Israel, Elijah challenged him to an open confrontation: my God versus your Baal—and whoever is left standing in the end is the True God. Ahab accepted. Before all the people, the Lord overwhelmed Baal. During the confrontation Elijah taunted the false prophets about Baal's impotency: "Shout louder! Surely he is a god! Perhaps he is deep in thought, or busy, or traveling. Maybe he is sleeping and must be awakened" (1 Kings 18:27). Elijah was aggressive, full of zeal for God's authority, seizing the opportunity not only to defeat Satan but also to demonstrate the lordship of Yahweh.

The key to the entire episode was Elijah's doing what God told him. He was a servant of God. "O Lord," he prayed, "God of Abraham, Isaac, and Israel, let it be known today that you are God in Israel and that I am your servant and have done all these things *at your command*" (1 Kings 18:36, emphasis mine). After this prayer, the fire of God fell, proving his presence. God's servant was vindicated. The response from the people was immediate: "The Lord—he is God! The Lord—he is God!"

Primitive peoples often need to see the superior power of the gospel demonstrated for them to believe. C. Peter Wagner received this report from Terrie L. Lillie, a student who documented it in a village in Kenya. It is told by an eyewitness whose primary language is not English.

A child was deadly sick in the same house after the end of the second week. She had malaria and surely she was dying. We were awakened at night by a big cry. We all ran to the direction of my grandmother's house. Kavili was crying, and Mbulu and the old woman, Kanini, the child born recently, was dying. She had changed her color and her eyes had turned completely white. There was no blinking.

Many more people were there and a lot more were coming. I got inside. Here was the people who did not know what to do and how to do it. I was as they were in the middle of the night, with no car or anything which could help anyone. No medicine was available at that time. Something had to be done. I thought it would be a good idea to pray and see what we would do next.

I asked to be given the child. I put her under my arms and called my wife to come near. I told everyone to come in that we may pray for the dying child. They came in but some feared that the child was going to die and so they did not go inside the house with a dead child. Then I had all of them sit. I began to pray. I did not make a long prayer. I said very few words. I simply asked the Lord to heal the child in the name of Jesus. Then I gave the child back to the mother.

The moment I gave it back, she was well. She was now breathing. She began to cry, she was nursed and she was well. Everyone took time to praise the name of the Lord. I could not really understand what was happening but I felt the power of God proceed out of me, and for a moment I did not want to say a lot of things. This was a big issue which made everyone present wonder to see how the Lord worked so quickly.

As a result of this instant, the whole village became Christians.

In this instance, a fatal illness needed to be overcome to open up the villagers to faith in Christ.

Alan Tippett describes an event in southern Polynesia that again illustrates the very human need to see the superior power of God actually demonstrated. In this case, a simple bump on a priestess's head released the tribe from years of fear and bondage to the false god Haehaetahi. Like Baal, Haehaetahi represents a religious system controlled by Satan.

> Peter Vi [a missionary] worked with the chief, teaching him the gospel. Eventually the chief, Taufa'ahau, reached the point where he felt he must begin to worship God. This demanded a dynamic encounter or confrontation with his old god, Haehaetahi.
>
> The priestess who served this god was much feared because she herself became the shrine of the deity under possession [of demons]. Taufa'ahau pulled a young banana tree and cut a club from the soft stalk. "I will strike the devil-god with this," he declared. On Vi's advice he removed the harder part of the root lest he kill the woman when he smote her under possession. At the moment when the priestess, under possession, was drinking the ceremonial kava, the chief struck her a blow on the forehead, which sent her rolling on the floor. Then before the drinking god had time to recover, the chief struck again and shouted a cry of victory that the god had been clubbed while drinking kava.[4]

The priestess was humiliated at losing her power. The people saw the victorious power of God, superior to the false god's power that had held them in fear and bondage. Because of this power encounter, they believed the gospel.

A WAR ZONE

An analogy that may help us understand what I mean by power encounter is found in nature. When warm and cold fronts collide, violence ensues: thunder and lightning, rain or snow—even tornadoes or hurricanes. There is conflict and a resulting release of energy. It is disorderly, messy, and difficult to control.

Power encounters are much like that. When the kingdom of God comes into direct contact with the kingdom of the world (when Jesus meets Satan), there is conflict. And usually it too is disorderly, messy, and difficult for us to control. The greatest instance of this was the crucifixion of Christ. At that moment an eternal sacrifice was made for us, so that our sin might be forgiven and the flesh, the world, and the devil might be utterly defeated. Great power was released that day. All of creation was rocked: the earth shook, rocks split, the sun stopped shining for three hours, and the Temple curtain was torn in two. Even tombs were opened, releasing the dead—"holy people" (Matt. 27:52). Life was radiating from the death of Christ; it shook a creation that was under the reign of evil. Two fronts, two kingdoms, two economies hit head on. And in the resurrection and ascension, Christ came out the victor, Satan the loser.

It was in this, the ultimate power encounter, that salvation was secured for all men and women who place their faith in Christ. But working that salvation out is another matter. In the present age, an interim period, before the coming of the fullness of the kingdom, the victory over Satan needs to be applied in the lives of people still under his power. Many Christians do not adequately recognize that though Christ's victory is irreversible, its application to everyday events is ongoing. Satan is still alive and well, even though his time on earth is limited.

German theologian Oscar Cullmann offers an analogy that helps us understand how, though defeated, Satan still has great power, power that can kill if left unchecked. In World War II, most military experts agree, victory for the Allies was assured on D-Day (June 6, 1944), the day they successfully invaded Nazi-occupied Europe on the Normandy beaches. Because Germany failed to prevent their entrance, victory for the British, American, and Canadian forces was inevitable. But it took eleven months for the Allies to actually end the war.

During this time thousands of men lost their lives in the bloodiest battles of the entire conflict. The coming V-E Day (May 8, 1945) was assured but not realized.[5] We are in a similar position as Christians: the final and full establishment of the kingdom of God, with Christ as its head, was assured at the resurrection, but we have yet to realize its fullness in the days in which we live.

We too are soldiers, members of Christ's army. Paul instructs Timothy, "Endure hardship with us like a good soldier of Christ Jesus" (2 Tim. 2:3). There is a war yet to be fought, an enemy still capable of inflicting great harm—if we allow him to. We must equip ourselves by allowing the power of the Spirit to come into our lives and work through us to defeat the enemy.

ONE NATION, ONE LANGUAGE

The unity of the early Christians was a crucial ingredient for their experiencing the power of the Spirit. In the book of Acts when Christians are described as being together in heart and mind, the power of God comes in extraordinary measure. They were "together in one place" (2:1), and Pentecost happened (2:2–13). They "devoted themselves to the apostles' teaching and to the fellowship" (2:42), and "many wonders and miraculous signs were done" (2:43). They "were one in heart and mind" (4:32), and "with great power the apostles continued to testify" (4:33).

In the second chapter we read of the birth of a warrior nation, the army of God, the church. In this nation we discover God's response to people's earlier attempt to unify as "one people speaking the same language" at the Tower of Babel (Gen. 11:1–9). Against the backdrop of the failure at Babel we learn a principle of spiritual unity from God's victory at Pentecost. At Babel, while observing the nations' attempt to make a name for themselves, the Lord said, "If as one people speaking the same language they have begun to do this, *then nothing they plan to do will be impossible* for them. Come, let us go down and confuse their language so they will not understand each other" (emphasis mine).

God readily acknowledges that power is present when people are united in purpose and language. Even the most rebellious and selfish people, when they come together, can accomplish much of what they set out to do. The potential for good *and* *evil* within men and women is almost boundless when they cooperate.

At Pentecost the Holy Spirit came to create a new nation from many nations, a new race from many races—the people of God (Acts 2:5–6, 41). Several words are used in Scripture to convey the meaning of a Christian nation. One of the most common Greek words for "nation" is *ethnos*. Karl Ludwig Schmidt, in the *Theological Dictionary of the New Testament*, says *ethnos* means a "multitude bound by the same manners, customs, or other distinctive features. It gives us the sense of a people."[6] If the "nations" of the world are always referred to as many, the "nation" of Christ is singular, a unit. This means that though a multitude, we are viewed by God as one people or society (see 1 Pet. 2:10; Gal. 3:6–9). This unity is one key to experiencing spiritual power.

One nation needs one language. At Pentecost God created order out of confusion, understanding of his word out of a multitude of languages. When the Holy Spirit came on the disciples, each of the others present heard them speak in his or her native tongue. Scripture describes the witnesses' initial response as being "amazed and perplexed" (Acts 2:12). That the disciples could speak in other languages was all the more remarkable because they were uneducated.

(As Galileans, the disciples probably had heavy accents. Though not expressly stated in the text, I believe that the disciples not only spoke other people's languages but also spoke them with their proper accents. This would be akin to someone with a thick Liverpool or Alabama accent speaking flawless Parisian French. Truly this would be a miracle.)

At Babel, one nation was broken into many, one language

changed to many, throwing everyone into confusion—resulting in a loss of power and purpose. At Pentecost, many nations and tongues were unified—and those present were able to experience an outpouring of power and three thousand new disciples were added (Acts 2:41).

Often in a power encounter that leads to conversion, the power of the Spirit appears first in those who are evangelizing, then in those who are evangelized. People at Pentecost were "amazed and perplexed." Many of them, though, took a quick step and crossed over to the other side: they became participants in God's grace. Often witnessing the presence of the Spirit in a Christian will open non-Christians to the gospel of the kingdom of God.

It took Peter's explanation of the phenomena at Pentecost to lead the three thousand to Christ. Usually, when non-Christians witness the power of the Spirit, they have many questions that only the gospel can answer. A rational explanation must be added to a transrational experience, the natural to the supernatural, for the most forceful advance of the kingdom of God.

An international army was born from the Pentecost power encounter. The remainder of Acts reads like war chronicles in which God's army does his bidding. Our lives should read the same way.

CHRISTIANS TOO

Power encounters are difficult to control and are therefore hard for many Western Christians to accept, because phenomena that do not fit rational thought are uncomfortable: they plunge us into the murky world of the transrational in which we lose control of the situation. Events that do not fit our normal categories of thinking are threatening for us, causing fear, because they are unfamiliar—especially where spiritual power is involved.

The first time I experienced a power encounter similar to

the one described at Pentecost, I became extremely irritated and angry at God. It was Mother's Day, 1979, and I had invited a young man to speak at the evening service of the church at which I had only recently become pastor, what would later become the Vineyard Christian Fellowship in Anaheim, California. His background was the California "Jesus People" movement of the late sixties and early seventies and, so I heard, he was unpredictable when he spoke. I was apprehensive about him, but I sensed God wanted him to speak nevertheless. He had been used by God to lead Christians into a refreshing experience of the Holy Spirit, and it was obvious to me that the congregation needed spiritual renewal. I hasten to point out that asking this young man to speak went contrary to my normal instincts as a pastor. I take seriously the admonition that pastors are to protect their flocks, but in this instance I sensed it was what God wanted. Regardless, I was to stand by the decision, whatever the cost.

When he eagerly agreed to speak, I became even more apprehensive. What will he say? What will he do to my church? The Lord gently reminded me, "Whose church is this?"

That evening he gave his testimony, a powerful story of God's grace. As he spoke, I relaxed. Nothing strange here, I thought. Then he did something that I had never seen done in a church gathering. He finished his talk and said, "Well, that's my testimony. Now the church has been offending the Holy Spirit a long time and it is quenched. So we are going to invite it to come and minister." We all waited. The air became thick with anticipation—and anxiety.

Then he said, "Holy Spirit, come." And it did!

(I must remind you that we were not a "Pentecostal" church with experience or understanding of the sorts of things that began to happen. What happened could not have been learned behavior.)

People fell to the floor. Others, who did not believe in tongues, loudly spoke in tongues. The speaker roamed among the crowd, praying for people, who then immediately fell over with the Holy Spirit resting on them.

I was aghast! All I could think throughout the experience was "Oh, God, get me out of here." In the aftermath, we lost church members and my staff was extremely upset. That night I could not sleep. Instead, I spent the evening reading Scripture, looking for the verse, "Holy Spirit, come." I never found it.

By 4:30 that morning I was more upset than I was earlier at the meeting. Then I remembered that I had read in *The Journal of John Wesley* about something like this happening. I went out to my garage and found a box of books about revivals and revivalists and began to read them. What I discovered was that our experience at the church service was not unique; people like John and Charles Wesley, George Whitefield, Charles Finney, and Jonathan Edwards all had similar experiences in their ministries. By 6:00 I had found at least ten examples of similar phenomena in church history.[7]

For example, on January 1, 1739, John Wesley wrote in his journal of an event on May 24, 1738:

Mr. Hall, Hinching, Ingham, Whitefield, Hutching and my brother Charles were present at our love feast in Fetter Lane with about 60 of our brethren. About three in the morning as we were continuing instant in prayer the power of God came mightily upon us, insomuch that many cried out for exulting joy and many fell to the ground. As soon as we were recovered a little from the awe and amazement at the presence of his Majesty, we broke out with one voice, "We praise thee O God, we acknowledge thee to be the Lord."[8]

Then I asked God for assurance that this was from him, that this was something he—not humans or Satan—was doing. Just after praying this prayer, the phone rang. Tom Stipe, a Denver, Colorado, pastor and good friend, called. I told him what had happened the night before, and he responded that it was from God. "That's exactly what happened in the early days of the Jesus People revival. Many people were saved." That conversation was significant, because Tom was a credible witness. I had only heard about these things; Tom had lived through them.

Over the next few months, supernatural phenomena continued to occur, frequently uninvited and without any encouragement, spontaneously. New life came into our church. All who were touched by and who yielded to the Holy Spirit—whether they fell over, started shaking, became very quiet and still, or spoke in tongues—accepted the experience and thought it was wonderful, drawing them closer to God. More importantly, prayer, Scripture reading, caring for others, and the love of God all increased.[9]

Our young people went out into the community, looking for people to evangelize and pray over. An event that I heard about is a good illustration of what often happened. One day a group of our young people approached a stranger in a parking lot. Soon they were praying over him, and he fell to the ground. By the time he got up, the stranger was converted. He is now a member of our church.

A revival began that May, and by September we had baptized over seven hundred new converts. There may have been as many as seventeen hundred new converts during a three-and-a-half-month period. I was an expert on church growth, but I had never seen evangelism like that.

Power encounters in the church, in this case without regard for "civilized propriety," catapulted us into all-out revival. What I had thought of as "order" in the twentieth-century church evidently was not the same as what Christians experienced in the New Testament church.

There is a word of caution, though. We would be mistaken to think that lack of order or organization allows the Holy Spirit greater freedom to work, while more order inhibits it. The right *kind* of order is necessary for the church to develop to maturity and fulfill its tasks. The church is an organism, a living body. A corpse is highly organized, but it is dead—it has no spirit within it. Many congregations are like corpses: wellordered but lacking the life of Christ. On the other hand, the one-celled amoeba, which certainly lacks organization and complexity, has life but can accomplish little. Prayer groups and other Christian organizations that reject the need for leadership are often like amoebas: they have life but are not able to accomplish much.

What God wants is a living body, where the Holy Spirit is free to operate and the body is ordered in such a manner that it can accomplish much. This body is quite complex, because the goal of evangelism and discipleship is an involved process. A key, though, is that God's order—not our own—be established. Sometimes he tips over our order so he can establish his.

FEARING GOD'S POWER

In Acts 5:12–16 we read of another response to power encounters: fear. "The apostles performed many miraculous signs and wonders among the people," this passage begins. In Jerusalem the apostles met daily at Solomon's Colonnade in the Temple, and the power of God came. At this time they were "highly regarded by the people." But the disciples were also feared, feared because people knew God was with them. "No one else dared join them," Scripture says.

Today many churches have become so secular—even profane—that nonmembers have no thought or concern about entering their premises. In fact, people often see the church as only another organization in need of their help. I frequently receive letters from secular fund-raising organizations offering to raise money for our church. For many, the church is an ineffective institution in need of expert advice—for a fee, of course.

In the New Testament, outsiders were afraid because they did not know what would happen to them if they moved in among Christians. They could be consumed by God's power; their secret sins could be revealed; healing could come to them; demons could be expulsed. Paul, writing to the Corinthians concerning the proper ordering of the spiritual gifts, instructs them to expect power encounters:

So if the whole church comes together and everyone speaks in tongues, and some who do not understand or some unbelievers come in, will they not say that you are out of your mind? But if an unbeliever or someone who does not understand comes in while everybody is prophesying, he will be convinced by all that he is a sinner and will be judged by all, and the secrets of his heart will be laid bare. So he will fall down and worship God, exclaiming, "God is really among you!" (1 Cor. 14:23–25).

God's Spirit works this way today. I recently read this anonymous account of a homosexual's conversion experience:

One weekend I went to visit some friends outside the city [in which he lived], people I knew from before my openly homosexual days. We had taken quite different directions—they were now Christians involved in the charismatic renewal—and I had never told them about my new life. However, I still enjoyed seeing them occasionally. In fact I was intrigued by their visible joy and fervor.

During this particular visit they asked me to go with them to a prayer meeting. I agreed, even though I expected an hour and a half of boredom. We drove through the steamy summer night to a large room crowded with people.

The meeting began with a few words from the leader and a couple of songs, followed by the low murmur of people praying aloud. It seemed things had barely begun when the leader was back on his feet, looking a little nervous. I can still hear him saying, "The Lord has told me that someone here tonight has been practicing homosexuality. He wants you to know that he loves you and forgives you."

That gentle message hit me like a thunderbolt. For years I had pushed the God of my childhood out of my mind. Now God was speaking to me. He wasn't just saying hello, either: he was asking me to give up my whole way of life.

I spent the rest of the meeting fighting with myself. "Why do I need forgiveness?" I would think. "I haven't done anything wrong." Then the religion lessons of my early years would come rushing back: who God was, what it meant that he loved me, what it meant to reject him. In the end, my debate boiled down to this: "I know enough about God to know that if he is speaking to me—and I believe he is—the only sensible thing for me to do is obey."

When the meeting ended, I turned to my friends. "That message was for me," I told them. "I want to do what God says."

* * *

Eventually I felt ready for marriage and fell in love with the woman who is now my wife. Our life together has been my most constant source of happiness.[10]

My coauthor, Kevin Springer, met the author of this testimony. Eight years after writing these words, he is still a strong Christian. He and his wife have three beautiful children. Reflecting on his conversion experience, he said, "For years before my conversion I was nervous around charismatics, uneasy that God might reveal my homosexuality to them. But by the time I attended the meeting at which I was converted, I was no longer on guard. So right when I let my guard down, God's power came on me."

OVERCOMING OPPOSITION

In Acts 13 we find a power encounter similar to the one between Elijah and the prophets of Baal. Paul and Barnabas, recently sent from the church at Antioch, were in the city of Paphos on the island of Cyprus. Word of their presence had come to Sergius Paulus, the Roman proconsul, and he sent for them "because he wanted to hear the word of God."

The scene is set for encounter between light and dark when Paul and Barnabas enter Sergius Paulus's chamber. Present was Elymas the sorcerer, opposing them with the purpose of turning the proconsul from his emerging faith. Jesus had his witness, Paul, and Satan his, Elymas.

There was need for action if Sergius Paulus was to be fully converted. Paul, filled with the Holy Spirit, took up the challenge. He said to Elymas, "You are a child of the devil and an enemy of everything that is right! You are full of all kinds of deceit and trickery. . . . Now the hand of the Lord is against you. You are going to be blind, and for a time you will be unable to see the light of the sun." At that moment Paul was speaking the words of God, under his unction. Elymas was immediately blinded.

And Sergius Paulus believed. Why? Because "he was amazed at the teaching about the Lord." What was the teaching? That the Lord was present, and was more powerful than anything in creation.

POWER AND MERCY

The Spirit can make its power felt in nature as well as through people. The result is often fear and openness in those seeing it. When Paul and Silas were thrown into the Philippian prison (they had been falsely accused of inciting a riot), God's power struck the prison, causing an earthquake, opening the doors, and loosening their chains (see Acts 16:16–40).

The jailer, who had fallen asleep, assumed the prisoners had fled. Roman guards who for any reason allowed their prisoners to escape were killed. So the jailer drew his sword to take his own life. But Paul stopped him. "Don't harm yourself! We are all here!"

Paul's response to God's power was mercy, mercy extended to the jailer. Instead of fleeing for their own lives, Paul and Silas stayed in the prison. The jailer rushed to them, fell down, and asked, "What must I do to be saved?" Paul replied, "Believe in the Lord Jesus, and you will be saved." The jailer and his household were saved, "and the whole family was filled with joy, because they had come to believe in God." When God's power is combined with his mercy, fearful hearts melt.

THE GREAT COMMISSION

We should not be surprised that the book of Acts is full of stories like these. At the end of Matthew's Gospel, Jesus commissions us to be sources of power encounters, ever ready to seize any opportunity to proclaim God's grace and mercy in order to make fully trained and obedient disciples. I believe the great commission can more effectively be fulfilled as we open our lives to God's power in the ways that I speak of in this book.

Before commanding us to "go and make disciples of all nations," Jesus prefaced his words with the statement: "All authority in heaven and on earth has been given me." *All* authority is in Christ, so anything that he commands us to do, we have access to the power required to do it.

The Greek word used here for authority is *exousia*. Theologian Werner Foerster notes that this word "denotes [Jesus'] divinely given power and authority to act. . . . It is his own rule in free agreement with the Father."[11] The Lord's Prayer to the Father was that "your kingdom come, your will be done on earth as it is in heaven" (Matt. 6:10). Jesus' entire life was built on the principle of doing the will of the Father, walking in his way and doing his works. "I tell you the truth," he told the Jews who were persecuting him, "the Son can do nothing by himself; he can do only what he sees his Father doing, because whatever the Father does the Son also does" (John 5:19).

All authority for making disciples is found in Christ, and he is with us today. "Surely I will be with you always, to the very end of the age," he assures us in the great commission (Matt. 28:20).

How is he with us? "All that belongs to the Father is mine. That is why I said the Spirit will take from what is mine and make it known to you" (John 16:15). It is the Holy Spirit, the "go-between God," who holds the key to power encounters. Our openness and availability to its direction and enabling, anointing, and power is the catalyst for fulfilling the great commission.

Clearly the early Christians had an openness to the power of the Spirit, which resulted in signs and wonders and church growth. If we want to be like the early church, we too need to open to the Holy Spirit's power.

3. Power Evangelism

It was the end of a long day of ministry and I was exhausted. I had just completed a teaching conference in Chicago and was flying off to another speaking engagement in New York. I was looking forward to the plane ride as a chance to relax for a few hours before plunging back into teaching. But it was not to be the quiet, uneventful trip I had hoped for.

Shortly after takeoff, I pushed back the reclining seat and readjusted the seat belt, preparing to relax. My eyes wandered around the cabin, not looking at anything in particular. Seated across the aisle from me was a middle-aged man, a business man, to judge from his appearance, but there was nothing unusual or noteworthy about him. But in the split second that my eyes happened to be cast in his direction, I saw something that startled me.

Written across his face in very clear and distinct letters I thought I saw the word "adultery." I blinked, rubbed my eyes, and looked again. It was still there. "Adultery." I was seeing it not with my eyes, but in my mind's eye. No one else on the plane, I am sure, saw it. It was the Spirit of God communicating to me. The fact that it was a spiritual phenomenon made it no less real.

By now the man had become aware that I was looking at him ("gaping at him" might be a more accurate description).

"What do you want?" he snapped.

As he spoke, a woman's name came clearly to mind. This was more familiar to me; I had become accustomed to the Holy Spirit bringing things to my awareness through these kinds of promptings.

Somewhat nervously, I leaned across the aisle and asked,

"Does the name Jane [not her real name] mean anything to you?"

His face turned ashen. "We've got to talk," he stammered.

The plane we were on was a jumbo jet, the kind with a small upstairs cocktail lounge. As I followed him up the stairs to the lounge, I sensed the Spirit speaking to me yet again. "Tell him if he doesn't turn from his adultery, I'm going to take him."

Terrific. All I had wanted was a nice, peaceful plane ride to New York. Now here I was, sitting in an airplane cocktail lounge with a man I had never seen before, whose name I didn't even know, about to tell him God was going to take his life if he didn't stop his affair with some woman.

We sat down in strained silence. He looked at me suspiciously for a moment, then asked, "Who told you that name?"

"God told me," I blurted out. I was too rattled to think of a way to ease into the topic more gracefully.

"*God* told you?" He almost shouted the question, he was so shocked by what I had said.

"Yes," I answered, taking a deep breath. "He also told me to tell you . . . that unless you turn from this adulterous relationship, he is going to take your life."

I braced myself for what I was sure would be an angry, defensive reaction, but to my relief the instant I spoke to him, his defensiveness crumbled and his heart melted. In a choked, desperate voice he asked me, "What should I do?"

At last I was back on familiar ground. I explained to him what it meant to repent and trust Christ and invited him to pray with me. With hands folded and head bowed, I began to lead him in a quiet prayer. "O God . . . "

That was as far as I got. The conviction of sin that had built up inside him seemed virtually to explode. Bursting into tears, he cried out, "O *God*, I'm so *sorry*" and launched into the most heartrending repentance I had ever heard.

It was impossible, in such cramped quarters, to keep hidden what was happening. Before long everyone in the cocktail lounge was intimately acquainted with this man's past sinfulness and present contrition. The flight attendants were even weeping right along with him.

When he finished praying and regained his composure, we talked for a while about what had happened to him.

"The reason I was so upset when you first mentioned that name to me," he explained, "was that my wife was sitting in the seat right next to me. I didn't want her to hear."

I knew he wasn't going to like what I said to him next.

"You're going to have to tell her."

"I am?" he responded weakly. "When?"

"Better do it right now," I said gently.

The prospect of confessing to his wife was, understandably, somewhat intimidating, but he could see there was no other way. So again I followed him, down the stairs and back to our seats.

I couldn't hear the conversation over the noise of the plane, but I could see his wife's stunned reaction, not only to his confession of infidelity, but also to his account of how the stranger sitting across the aisle had been sent by God to warn him of the consequences of his sin. Eyes wide with amazement (and probably terror!), she stared first at her husband, then at me, then back at her husband, then back at me, as the amazing story unfolded. In the end the man led his wife to accept Christ, right there on the airplane.

There was little time to talk when we got off the airplane in New York. They didn't own a Bible, so I gave them mine. Then we went our separate ways.

This might seem like an unusual, if not bizarre, event, yet I could write hundreds of other accounts like it—both from my own experience and from that of others I know. I call this type of encounter *power evangelism*, and I believe it was one of the most effective means of evangelism in the early church.[1] Further, power evangelism appears to have been present during periods of great missionary expansion and renewal throughout church history (see Appendix A).

By power evangelism I mean a presentation of the gospel that is rational but that also transcends the rational. The explanation of the gospel comes with a demonstration of God's power through signs and wonders. Power evangelism is a spontaneous, Spirit-inspired, empowered presentation of the gospel. Power evangelism is evangelism that is preceded and undergirded by supernatural demonstrations of God's presence. Through these supernatural encounters people experience the presence and power of God. Usually this takes the form of words of knowledge (such as were given to me about the man on the airplane), healing, prophecy, and deliverance from evil spirits. In power evangelism, resistance to the gospel is overcome by the demonstration of God's power in supernatural events, and receptivity to Christ's claims is usually very high.

Many of us are suspicious of a story in which supernatural knowledge of personal sin is used in evangelism. This demonstrates how far Christianity in Western society has drifted from experiences that were everyday occurrences in New Testament times. Yet if power evangelism is a normal type of evangelism and Western Christians rarely experience it, this exclusion will be reflected in the results of our evangelistic efforts.

WHO IS EVANGELIZING WHOM?

Are the Christian churches effective in evangelism today? Jesus told his disciples, "The harvest is plentiful but the workers are few" (Matt. 9:37). In the West the number of workers in domestic (and foreign) missions has been increasing for the past fifteen years, especially among evangelicals. (We would be mistaken to think that only missionaries or full-time Christian leaders are the "workers" Christ was calling for. *Every* Christian has been called to the harvest. However, an increase in the number of professional workers without a corresponding increase in the harvest indicates that there is another factor responsible for the waning of Christianity in Western culture.)

English and American domestic missionary organizations such as Campus Crusade for Christ, the Navigators, Inter-Varsity Christian Fellowship, and countless evangelical denominational groups are more active now than at any time in their history. Programs like Evangelism Explosion, Luis Palau Crusades, and Campus Crusade's "Here's Life" have growing staffs. Though there is always a need for more workers, there has never been a time in this century when so many workers and programs have been tilling the fields.

Taking into consideration the increase in domestic missionary activity in recent years, one would expect an improved church life. One indicator of the level of church life (and indirectly the effectiveness of evangelization efforts) is church attendance. In England less than ten percent of the population regularly attend church. In the United States, a country not as secularized as England, church participation is much higher. Currently forty-two percent of the U.S. population attend a worship service in a typical week, and sixty-eight percent are enrolled in churches (140,816,358 people reported in 1984). These numbers nevertheless represent a steady downward trend in attendance over the past fifteen years.[2]

More significantly, those who do claim to be Christians are not living effective, fully converted lives. Commenting on the problem, author Joseph Bayly notes, "I don't think any observer would dispute the fact that the evangelical Protestant subculture has been overrun by the general American culture's values. If divorce rates have risen in the general culture, they have also risen among evangelical Protestants. . . . [They] follow a similar pattern of TV viewing, of materialism, and other cultural changes."[3] In fact, according to recent studies conducted by the National Opinion Research Center, the percentage of those married who have been divorced or legally separated is higher among U.S. Protestants than in the general population.[4]

George Gallup in his report "1984 Religion in America" was more stinging in his observation of the level of Christian living in the United States: "Religion is growing in importance among

Americans but morality is losing ground. . . . There is very little difference in the behavior of the churched and unchurched on a wide range of items including lying, cheating, and pilferage."

There could be other explanations for these discouraging figures and observations. For example, they could also indicate that the world is more effectively "evangelizing" Christians than we are evangelizing the world. In other words, the figures could point to increased secularization trends within the church, which is not necessarily an indictment of our missionary methods.

More significantly, these figures could also indicate there are problems not with the methods so much as with the message: a "cheap grace" gospel is frequently preached, producing weak Christians who do not stand when powerful and persuasive attacks come from the world. I believe this is a serious problem; many Christians do not understand or know how to communicate the gospel of the kingdom of God.

I am not implying that all Western evangelical methods of evangelism are ineffective. Denominations like the Christian and Missionary Alliance, the Church of the Nazarene, and the Southern Baptists, which generally oppose the charismatic gifts, have experienced impressive growth in recent years. But on a worldwide scale, an estimated seventy percent of all church growth is among Pentecostal and charismatic groups.

Better indicators of the effectiveness of Western evangelical methodologies are studies of specific programs. Dr. Win Arn, writing in the January–February 1977 issue of *Church Growth America*, reports on several programs, including Campus Crusade for Christ's "Here's Life America," a media and phone contact program. Of the West Morris Street Free Methodist Church in Indianapolis, Indiana, which participated in a "Here's Life" campaign, Dr. Arn writes: "In researching the facts with Pastor Riggs we found . . . that the church made over 6,000 phone calls . . . 362 people made a decision . . . and 20 attended one or more Bible studies. When I asked how many of those who had made decisions were now (five months later) members of the church, the answer was 'Zero.' Effective evangelism? Hardly."

C. Peter Wagner, writing in the September 1977 issue of *Eternity* magazine, offers even more conclusive figures on the "Here's Life America" program. He gathered data from 178 participating churches in six cities. These are the results:

26,535 gospel presentations
4,106 decisions for Christ
526 people came to a Bible study
125 new church members

While the 4,106 figure is impressive, the people do not appear to be fully converted. They lack the convincing fruit of discipleship in their lives: they do not go with Bible study and church membership, both reliable indicators of effective evangelism.

In the January–February 1978 issue of *Church Growth America*, Dr. Arn reports on results from the 1976 Seattle-Tacoma Billy Graham Crusade. Out of 434,100 persons who attended, there were 18,000 decisions for Christ registered. Out of those 18,000 only 1,285 people were finally incorporated into a local church.

While these statistics are more encouraging than those for "Here's Life America," they still do not indicate effective evangelism.

Both Billy Graham and Campus Crusade for Christ are aware of these statistics, and they have taken steps to improve on them. For example, Eddie Gibbs, a professor at Fuller Seminary, helped develop a follow-up program to Billy Graham's 1984 England crusade, and early statistics indicate a much higher percentage of people are joining local churches and Bible studies than in previous crusades. Campus Crusade now employs men and women trained in principles of church growth developed by Donald McGavran and C. Peter Wagner.

Most evangelism practiced in the West lacks the power seen

in New Testament evangelism. Although there is always need for more workers to reap the harvest, the current situation in Western societies indicates a need also for more powerful ways for those workers to reach people with the gospel.

IT'S A WESTERN PROBLEM

You will notice that I said that the need for effective evangelism is greatest in Western societies; in many non-Western (usually Third World) countries, this does not appear to be the case. C. Peter Wagner was a missionary in Bolivia for sixteen years. Here is what he learned about growing churches in Latin societies:

My background is that of a Scofield Bible dispensational evangelical. I was taught that the gifts of the Spirit were not in operation in our age; they went out with the apostolic church. . . . [Even today] I see myself neither a charismatic nor a Pentecostal. . . . I began looking around and trying to get a handle on church growth in Latin America. Much to my surprise I began discovering that the churches that were far outgrowing all the others were the Pentecostal churches.

While I lived in Bolivia I traveled quite a bit to Chile and studied the Pentecostal movement there. The understanding I got through the Chilean Pentecostals began to open me to the validity of signs, wonders, healings, and tongues in our day and age.

His conclusion regarding the key to effective evangelism is remarkable, especially when it is kept in mind that Dr. Wagner is not a "classical" Pentecostal:

What I'm seeing, as the picture is beginning to emerge, is that worldwide there is a remarkably close relationship between growth of the churches today and the healing ministry—particularly, but not exclusively, in new areas where the gospel has just penetrated, where the devil has had complete reign for centuries or millennia. When the gospel first penetrates a region, if we don't go in with an understanding of and use of the supernatural power of the Holy Spirit, we just don't make much headway. . . .

[For example,] in Brazil 40 percent of the population are practicing spiritists and another 40 percent have had some direct experience with it. The way the gospel is spreading there is by a confrontration: healings, miracles, signs, and wonders.[5]

Another example of what Dr. Wagner describes is the Full Gospel Central Church, located in Seoul, Korea. Launched on May 18, 1958, under the direction of Dr. Paul Yonggi Cho, the church today has over five hundred thousand members, and seventeen thousand members are being added each month! It is unquestionably the world's largest local church.

"My mind drifts back to the beginning days of the church, known even then for a constant flow of God's miracle power," says Dr. John Hurston, who has been with the Full Gospel Central Church since its beginning. He was responding to a question about the reason for its phenomenal growth: "Perhaps the answer . . . is the continuation of a trend modeled by Christ: 'People brought to Jesus many who had demons in them. Jesus drove out the evil spirits with a word and healed all who were sick' " (Matt. 8:16).

Power evangelism is flourishing in nontechnological countries. People living in these countries are often animists; that is, they believe there are actual spirits that hold people in bondage and the supernatural power of the Holy Spirit is needed to break their hold. A colleague of mine from Fuller Theological Seminary, Dr. Charles Kraft, tells about going to Nigeria and attempting to teach the book of Romans to a small tribe. After a few months, they came to him very politely and said that they appreciated his teaching but it was not relevant to their needs. What they needed was wisdom for dealing with spirits that plagued the villagers every night, something that Kraft readily admitted he was not trained to do. Under such circumstances it is not surprising that more than half of all American foreign missionaries return home after only one tour.[6]

We would be mistaken to think that power evangelism was needed only in countries with less technological cultures. In

Western culture, because of the influence of materialism and rationalism, many people do not believe in a spirit world, or if they do, they do not believe or live as though the spirit world could affect the material world. But their unbelief does not exclude demonic activity from our societies; demons' existence is not dependent on our belief in them. A mind-set that excludes the possibility of direct intervention by supernatural powers (good or bad) in the world makes Christians vulnerable to Satan.

Because Western Christians are inhibited from practicing power evangelism, their effectiveness is blunted. This leaves them ineffective in dealing with people who have problems with demons, illness, and serious sin.

In 1974 I resigned as co-pastor of Yorba Linda Friends Church to become founding department head of the Department of Church Growth at what is now called the Charles E. Fuller Institute of Evangelism and Church Growth in Pasadena, California. At the same time I began an adjunct professorship at the School of World Mission–Institute of Church Growth, Fuller Theological Seminary. Working with men like Donald A. McGavran (who is recognized worldwide as the father of the church growth movement), C. Peter Wagner, and Charles Kraft, I became familiar with the practice of power evangelism in Third World countries, particularly with reports of signs and wonders and dramatic church growth. These reports caught my attention.

At the same time I traveled extensively across the United States, in a four-year period working with thousands of pastors from twenty-seven denominations (none Pentecostal or charismatic), speaking about church growth and evangelism. The contrast between churches on the mission field and in America was striking: Most American churches lacked both power encounters and the dramatic growth so common in other parts of the world.

When I left the pastorate in 1974 I thought I would never return. I could no longer lead an institution that I had many questions about. My subsequent travels around the country did little to change many of my negative impressions of many American evangelical churches.

But in 1978 God spoke to me about returning to the pastorate. Through the credible, intelligent testimony of Pentecostal professors like Russell Spittler, through the reports of signs and wonders from Third World students and missionaries, and through a greater understanding of how Western materialism undermines Christians' acceptance of the supernatural, I began to open my heart to the Holy Spirit. I wondered if signs and wonders and church growth like those in Third World countries were possible in the United States. I would have to become a pastor again to find out.

So with much apprehension and the encouragement of my wife and Peter Wagner, I resigned my position at the Institute of Evangelism and Church Growth and returned to the pastorate, a wayward shepherd coming to serve a tiny flock. Unlike the first time I pastored, this time I had a clear sense of mission: to prove whether the signs and wonders and church growth being reported by Fuller Seminary Third World students was possible in the United States.

We started with about fifty people at home meetings in which we worshiped God, studied Scripture, sang, and prayed. By our second year we had grown to over two hundred members and were meeting in a high-school gymnasium. (Later we took on the name Vineyard Christian Fellowship.) In our first year we did not experience the signs and wonders described in the New Testament. Therefore, I began a series of sermons from the Gospel of Luke. Luke is full of the healing ministry of Jesus; I was forced to begin teaching on the subject. I thought, what better place to start than with the healing ministry?

Soon I was praying for the sick, not because I had seen the sick healed but because that was what Scripture teaches Christians to do. Over the course of the next ten months, week in and week out, I prayed for people—and not one person was healed. Half of the members left the church. I kept preaching and praying about healing because during this period (when I wanted to quit) God spoke clearly to me: "Do not preach your experience. Preach my word." Though I continued to sound foolish because of my lack of results, I did not stop preaching about God's desire to heal today. (I was not claiming that people were being healed who were in fact not healed, only that, based on the Bible, more people should be healed.)

During this time the Lord taught me several things. First, it took months for me to realize that if an experience such as healing was commonly found in Scripture yet not a part of my experience, something was wrong with how I approached it. Before, I had assumed that God didn't hear me.

I assumed that Scripture study, especially as approached in evangelical seminaries, was the key to being equipped and empowered to do God's work. In fact, I was to learn that there was more to being equipped than learning about the Bible. I still believe in the importance and necessity of education, but I no longer see it as the sole avenue to being equipped and empowered to do God's work.

Second, I became aware of different types of faith and how often I did not seek faith for miracles. As an evangelical I thought of personal Christian growth as having two components, doctrinal faith and faithfulness. Doctrinal faith comes as we grow in understanding right doctrine or correct teaching. We know that we are growing in doctrinal faith as we grow intellectually in knowledge about God, his nature, character, how he acts, and so on. Faithfulness is character growth or the development of the fruit of the Spirit in our lives (Gal. 5:22–23). And essentially I found that to be true, but incomplete.

Through this ten-month period I became aware of another dimension of Christian growth, an exercise of faith for miracles such as healing, words of knowledge, and so on. (Perhaps this is the "faith" described in 1 Cor. 12:9.) Key to this was learning how to know when God's unction or anointing had come for a task like healing in a particular situation.

Emphasis on doctrinal knowledge and character development is good; this other dimension of Christian growth adds
much more. This was a difficult lesson for me to learn, which
explains why nothing happened for many months.

At the end of this ten-month period, when I was at my
lowest point, a woman was healed. Her husband had called
and asked me to come pray for her—she was very ill. The
healing occurred after I prayed for her and had begun a well-
rehearsed explanation to her husband about why she probably
wouldn't be healed. During my explanation she got out of bed
completely whole again. This was the beginning of a trickle
that soon became a steady stream.

Today we see hundreds of people healed every month in
Vineyard Christian Fellowship services. Many more are healed
as we pray for them in hospitals, on the streets, and in homes.
The blind see; the lame walk; the deaf hear. Cancer is
disappearing.

Most importantly for me as a pastor, the people are taking
healing and other supernatural gifts to the streets, leading
many who otherwise would not be open to the message of the
gospel to Christ. I estimate that twenty percent of our people
regularly see someone healed through their prayers. The gifts
are not confined to church services; they are tools employed
in reaching the lost.

D. Martyn Lloyd-Jones, in a book taken from his lectures,
Joy Unspeakable, points out that in the book of Acts the relationship between the anointing of the Holy Spirit and evangelism
is striking: "Go through Acts and in every instance when we
are told either that the Spirit came upon these men or that
they were filled with the Spirit, you will find that it was in
order to bear a witness and a testimony."[7]

Since 1978 the Vineyard Christian Fellowships have grown
to include one hundred and forty congregations, mostly in the
United States and England, with over forty thousand members. The majority of our members are new converts (mostly
young people) who experienced a power encounter.

Vineyard Christian Fellowships are not the only churches that have discovered power evangelism. Others like St. Andrew's Anglican Church in Chorleywood, Herts, England; Gateway Baptist Church in Boswell, New Mexico; Crenshaw Christian Center in Los Angeles, California; and Our Lady of Perpetual Help in Boston, Massachusetts, have all experienced remarkable growth, both in number as well as in the maturity of their members. Each has an ongoing ministry of signs and wonders.

Power evangelism is not excluded from any culture. We have seen that it can flourish in Western societies with the same results that occurred in the first century or that are reported from Africa, South and Central America, and Asia today.

POWER VERSUS PROGRAM

Over the past seven years, as I have seen the outstanding response to power evangelism, I have reflected on the reasons for its success, especially when compared to contemporary Western evangelistic efforts, most of which I call programmatic evangelism. A comparison of the two shows significant differences.

Programmatic evangelism attempts to reach the minds and hearts of people without the aid of charismatic gifts. Programmatic evangelism is usually characterized by message-centered communicators who present the gospel primarily through rational arguments. In some cases an appeal to the emotions is also employed. Usually it is one-way communication, a prepared message given by the speaker to passive listeners. There is also an emphasis on organization and technique, a search for the one most effective presentation of the gospel, and the tacit assumption that if people understand the propositions of the gospel they will decide to become Christians. Of course, there is also the valid assumption that in its proclamation the gospel has intrinsic power.

Programmatic evangelism comes in many forms; organized

crusades or revivals, door-to-door saturation campaigns in which tracts are presented, media campaigns, personal evangelism contacts, and friendship evangelism are only a few examples. In each of these the heart of the evangelistic task is a presentation of several steps needed to enter a relationship with Christ. These steps are not an adumbration of intellectual arguments for the gospel. They are a simple presentation of the steps to salvation, which is good. But an assumption in almost all programmatic evangelism is that reservations in a potential convert are usually intellectual in nature; thus a high emphasis is placed on answering theological objections.

By its very nature and assumptions, programmatic evangelism tends to have as its goal decisions for Christ, not disciples. Many people who make these decisions do not encounter God's power; thus frequently do not move on to a mature faith. Because there is something inadequate about their conversion experience, later growth for many is retarded.

In programmatic evangelism, Christians witness to everyone they meet, in obedience to the general command of Scripture to "go and make disciples." In power evangelism the same command is obeyed, only differently. Each evangelism experience is initiated by the Holy Spirit for a *specific* place, time, person, or group. Instead of indiscriminately spreading the message and depending on a preprogrammed message, those practicing power evangelism depend on the immediate illumination of the Holy Spirit to give pertinent information for each encounter.

In programmatic evangelism, the Christian says, "In obedience I go. Holy Spirit bless me." In power evangelism, the Christian says, "As the Holy Spirit tells me to go, I go."

In programmatic evangelism, Christians might be fearful as they speak, but they are not unsure about *what* they are going to say before opening their mouths. In power evangelism, Christians are consciously under God's commission and control. They too are fearful as they speak, but they are far more *vulnerable* than those in programmatic evangelism because they cannot depend on a prepackaged message. (Fear of losing control is threatening to most Western Christians, something I will comment on further in Chapter 5.)

In programmatic evangelism the attitude is that we do something and then God works. In power evangelism, God speaks and then we act.

My contention is not that programmatic evangelism has been wrong. After all, power evangelism employs the heart of programmatic evangelism, a simple presentation of the gospel. Programmatic evangelism has been responsible for bringing millions of people to a personal relationship with Christ. I encourage the practice and development of new kinds of programmatic evangelism. Power evangelism is a catalyst in the programmatic task. My point is that programmatic evangelism is often incomplete, lacking demonstration of the kingdom of God in signs and wonders—but this in no way invalidates the gospel presentation.

C. Peter Wagner in his book *Frontiers in Missionary Strategy* introduces a paradigm that describes different goals of evangelism. I have found his model very helpful for understanding how power evangelism and programmatic evangelism help or hinder meeting those goals. Dr. Wagner describes three styles of evangelism based on different goals: presence evangelism, proclamation evangelism, and persuasion evangelism.

Presence evangelism is the witness of good works and good deeds (Matt. 5:16). These are not supernatural works such as healing or deliverance from evil spirits; instead, they are acts of mercy, generosity, and aid to the poor. The effectiveness of this style of evangelism is measured by how many people are being helped in the name of the Lord. Dr. Wagner calls this "good evangelism."

Proclamation evangelism adds good words to good deeds. The goal here is to help people hear and respond to the gospel (Rom. 10:14–15). The emphasis is on helping people make a decision to love Christ.

Persuasion evangelism, Dr. Wagner says, is the best style of evangelism, because it takes people from the decision phase to the disciple phase. This is the goal of evangelism that Christ calls us to in the great commission passage of Matthew (28:19–20). By disciple phase Wagner means becoming fully *incorporated* into the body of Christ (in a local church). This includes being *taught* the basics of the word of God and *trained* in a Christian way of living that affects every area of a person's life; the person is then *enabled* to do God's works on earth. In sum, the goal of discipleship is that we become, to use C. S. Lewis's term, "little Christs"[8]—that we take on his character and do his works.

I have discovered that there are many Christians who believe persuasion evangelism is God's ideal, but they do not know how to lead people beyond the decision stage. They are frustrated in their efforts to make disciples. Most of the programmatic efforts, because of their emphasis on rational decisions, only help people along to the proclamation phase. The methodology and content of programmatic evangelism frequently are insufficient to lead people into the persuasion, or discipleship, stage.

A key to moving from presence to proclamation to persuasion evangelism is employing power evangelism, the demonstration of God's power through signs and wonders. Power evangelism is a catalyst for accelerating the transition through the various phases. In power evangelism key obstacles—an adulterous affair, bitterness, a physical ailment, demon possession—are exposed and overcome, striking deeply into the hearts of people. This frees new believers from major obstacles so that they may experience future spiritual growth. Further, power encounters authenticate conversion experiences in a way that mere intellectual assents do not. This gives new Christians confidence about their conversion, a solid foundation for the rest of their lives.

It is Christ's presence and power that make it possible for people to become mature disciples, to do his works. Without his power we cannot lead people into the discipleship phase.

A REVEALING QUESTION

Shortly after Jesus raised from the dead a man in the city of Nain, John the Baptist sent two of his disciples to ask him, "Are you the one who was to come, or should we expect someone else?" (Luke 7:19). Jesus did not reply by giving a set of logical proofs in the manner to which we are accustomed. Instead, he validated his ministry from the perspective of a power demonstration of the kingdom of God. Jesus demonstrated that he was the Messiah by the works he did that fulfilled the Old Testament messianic prophecies. (In this sense, there is logic and rationality to his response to John's disciples.) "Go back and report to John what you have seen and heard: The blind receive sight, the lame walk, those who have leprosy are cured, the deaf hear, the dead are raised, and the good news is preached to the poor." Jesus was telling the disciples to reassure John by what they had seen and heard— the healing of the sick, the expulsion of evil spirits, and the raising of the dead.

These were not sporadic events in Christ's ministry. A close look at Scripture reveals that Jesus spent more time healing and casting out demons than preaching. Out of 3,774 verses in the four Gospels, 484 (12 percent of the total) relate specifically to the healing of physical and mental illness and the resurrection of the dead. Except for discussion about miracles in general, attention devoted to the healing ministry of Jesus is far greater than that devoted to any other aspect of his ministry. John's disciples would have understood from Old Testament prophets like Isaiah that the presence of the Messiah—the embodiment of the kingdom of God—was demonstrated in power encounters. The early church was effective because it understood evangelism as a testimony that Christ was the fulfillment of the promise of the Messiah, with powerful demonstrations of the kingdom of God that confirmed his message.

"As the Father has sent me," said Jesus to the disciples after his resurrection, "I am sending you." He then breathed the Holy Spirit on them (John 20:21, 22). Earlier, after challenging Thomas to believe in him on the basis of his miracles, he had said, "Anyone who has faith in me will do what I have been doing. He will do even greater things than these . . . " (John 14:11, 12). Clearly Jesus envisioned a group of people—his disciples—who would perform not only the same but even greater miracles than he did. The only hindrance to receiving this power is lack of faith: "*Anyone* who has faith in me . . . " It was Christ's intention that the kingdom of God be spread by others in the same way that he did it—through power evangelism.

Paul's understanding of this perspective accounted for his phenomenal success in Corinth. This understanding came after only a modest response in Athens. In Athens Paul argued eloquently at the Areopagus, with the results that "a *few* men became followers of Paul and believed" (Acts 17:34). Many Western Christians use Paul's sermon as a model for modern evangelistic efforts, ignoring its meager results.

In Corinth, the next stop on his apostolic tour, the results were that "*many* people in this city" believed (Acts 18:10). While there are several factors that explain the different responses (particularly the different degrees of receptivity found in the people of each city), Paul himself wrote to those in Corinth, "When I came to you, brothers, I did not come with eloquence or superior wisdom. . . . My message and my preaching were not with wise and persuasive words, but with a demonstration of the Spirit's power, so that your faith might not rest on men's wisdom, but on God's power" (1 Cor. 2:1, 4, 5). Paul changed his evangelistic methods: in Corinth he combined demonstration with proclamation.

4. The Divine Appointment

It had been a long day at the office, full of deadlines and meetings that leave editors eager for only one thing: getting home and relaxing with their families. As Kerry Jennings (not his real name) navigated across the freeway system toward his suburban home, he fell into prayer, a habit he had developed to redeem the hours spent in traffic jams. He interceded for his family, his co-workers, and his friends. He prayed about an article that he was writing. Then he began asking God to provide opportunities for personal evangelism. Suddenly strange thoughts entered his mind, as well as the accompanying peace indicating the Lord was responding to his prayers. He had acted on these kinds of thoughts before, almost always seeing God work through him.

God told Kerry to stop at a familiar restaurant, look for a certain waitress, and tell her that "God had something for her." Further, God said that what he had for the waitress would be revealed when Kerry talked with her. Though apprehensive, Kerry responded to the instruction, steering his car toward the restaurant.

He did so because he sensed that God had arranged a divine appointment. A *divine appointment* is an appointed time in which God reveals himself to an individual or group through spiritual gifts or other supernatural phenomena. God arranges these encounters—they are meetings he has ordained to demonstrate his kingdom (Eph. 2:10).

After being seated in the waitress's section, Kerry began to ponder all the reasons for not delivering the message. While he was caught up in anxious thoughts, she approached. Before he could say anything, she cheerfully said, "You have something for me, don't you?" In response (his resistance was now gone), he told her that God had sent him specifically with something, and then two insights regarding her job and a relationship (both areas of trouble for her) were supernaturally revealed to him. Asking God for courage, he told her.

She was stunned. She knew that she was encountering God, because the only way Kerry could have known the things he told her was through supernatural means. (In Scripture this is called "a word of knowledge" or "message of knowledge"; see 1 Cor. 12:8.) At the end of the conversation they prayed. She cried. Later Kerry learned that she was the daughter of a Christian pastor, now deceased, and that she had turned away from God. Soon after the divine appointment she gave her heart to God.

Divine appointments are an integral part of power evangelism. People who would otherwise resist hearing the gospel are instantly opened to God's word. Sometimes even the most hostile individuals turn to God when a significant need is met.

SERENDIPITY

"Always be prepared to give an answer to everyone who asks you to give the reason for the hope that you have" (1 Pet. 3:15); that is, every Christian should always be prepared to proclaim the way of salvation. Yet what I am describing in divine appointments goes beyond the simple explanation of the gospel. While proclamation is an important element of divine appointments, it would be misleading to think of them only as opportunities to explain the way of salvation.

For example, in Luke 19:1–10, we find the story of Jesus coming through the town of Jericho. His encounter with Zacchaeus, the short and unpopular tax collector, is an excellent illustration of a divine appointment. On seeing him, Jesus said, "Zacchaeus, come down immediately. Today I must stay at your house." Then Zacchaeus said, "Look, Lord! Here and now I give half of my possessions to the poor, and if I have cheated anybody out of anything, I will pay back four times the amount." What could explain Zacchaeus's remarkable response to such a simple request?

First, Jesus called him by name. There is no indication in Scripture that Jesus had any prior knowledge of Zacchaeus. Jesus was doing here what the Holy Spirit enables Christians to do through a word of knowledge, what Kerry Jennings did when he spoke to the waitress. Second, Zacchaeus was hated by the townspeople; as tax collector he took from the Jews on behalf of the Romans, keeping everything (which was usually a considerable sum of money) that exceeded the Roman requirements. He was a man who probably had few friends. He had a deep need for acceptance and human companionship. Jesus reached out to him and communicated through a simple request for hospitality that he loved and accepted him.

Supernatural revelation. The meeting of a deep human need. It is small wonder that Zacchaeus was saved (probably before his feet hit the ground as he jumped from the tree), that all resistance to the gospel was overcome.

There are other lessons to learn from the story of Zacchaeus as well. Many times, God works miracles in quite different ways from what we expect. Zacchaeus climbed the tree in order to see Christ more clearly, but in doing so was himself more clearly seen by God. In this regard, divine appointments have an air of serendipity about them, a surprising discovery of divine favor.

Illustrations of supernatural, transrational encounters like this in Scripture are not exceptional. Another example, perhaps the most striking in the Bible, is the calling of Nathanael in the first chapter of John's Gospel.

Too often Western Christians evangelize with a mind-set that omits the supernatural. We operate with this mind-set because we are unaware of the supernatural promptings of the Holy Spirit. Have you ever experienced promptings or thoughts similar to those of Kerry Jennings, only to dismiss them as the result of a bad cup of coffee? Have you ever experienced flashes of insight when talking to someone that you knew what his or her problem or need was before that person told you, only to later dismiss it as lucky intuition? If so, perhaps from now on you should more attentively listen for God's voice, stepping out in faith when you sense his promptings.

THE PROCESS OF CONVERSION

Evangelism is a complex process in which the Holy Spirit works in the hearts and minds of people. Central to the process is communication. Viggo Sogaard offers a model (developed at a 1970 seminar in Bangkok) of the various stages that people frequently go through in coming to full maturity in Christ (the letters are not labels for the successive stages; they are meant to show a progression or scale only).

S A Knows absolutely nothing about the gospel
O
W D Had initial exposure to the gospel
I
N G Understands some basic characteristics of the gospel
G
      J Understands implications of the gospel and way of salvation
R M
E
A N
P   Decision
I   O
N
G R

R   New Christian
E U
F   Mature Christian and layleader
I
N X Mature and trained leader who is able to teach others
I
N
G Z

In commenting on his model, Sogaard says, "It should be noted that the model indicates stages, which themselves are processes. Reaping is indicated as a process, and the model has a 'conversion point' only for the sake of illustration. The decision point could be at almost any point on the scale, but experience indicates that conversions that are genuine and lasting usually take place after a person has understood the basic characteristics of the gospel. Conversions would therefore usually take place in the area indicated as reaping."[1] The goal of the evangelism process is moving people along the scale from A to Z, not only to a personal conversion experience but also to maturity in Christ.

But this model for understanding the conversion process is deficient. A second dimension, people's attitudes, is also significant in the process. James F. Engel in his "Engel Scale" draws from secular research on attitudes in business and politics to show how attitudes affect the evangelism process.[2] The Engel Scale integrates knowledge, belief, attitude, intention, and decision making to help us understand conversion. (C. Peter Wagner adds to the Engel Scale stages of discipleship training and witnessing in word and life-style for Christ.)

The Engel Scale is an easy model to understand, and most Christians can quickly place those with whom they are talking on the scale so they can better understand their needs. Once this is done, the gospel message can be adapted to where the person is in thinking and attitude, to his or her needs.

Most Christians unaware of the Engel Scale move non-Christians along this scale haphazardly. For example, if we talk with a person that barely has an awareness that there is a Supreme Being (-8 on the Engel Scale) in the same way as with someone who grasps the personal implications of the gospel (-5), we will speak a message he or she cannot understand. Programmatic evangelism, because it is a planned presentation, inclines Christians toward approaching all non-Christians as though they are at the same place in the conversion process. Of course, poor or no training in personal evangelism also

SPIRITUAL-DECISION PROCESS

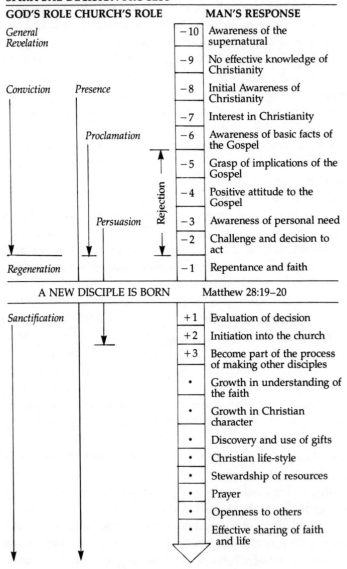

GOD'S ROLE	CHURCH'S ROLE		MAN'S RESPONSE
General Revelation		−10	Awareness of the supernatural
		−9	No effective knowledge of Christianity
Conviction	*Presence*	−8	Initial Awareness of Christianity
		−7	Interest in Christianity
	Proclamation	−6	Awareness of basic facts of the Gospel
		−5	Grasp of implications of the Gospel
		−4	Positive attitude to the Gospel
	Persuasion	−3	Awareness of personal need
		−2	Challenge and decision to act
Regeneration		−1	Repentance and faith

A NEW DISCIPLE IS BORN   Matthew 28:19–20

Sanctification		+1	Evaluation of decision
		+2	Initiation into the church
		+3	Become part of the process of making other disciples
		•	Growth in understanding of the faith
		•	Growth in Christian character
		•	Discovery and use of gifts
		•	Christian life-style
		•	Stewardship of resources
		•	Prayer
		•	Openness to others
		•	Effective sharing of faith and life

(Rejection)

Adapted from "What's Gone Wrong With The Harvest?" by James F. Engel and Wilbert Norton—Zondervan 1975.

contributes to Christians' incorrectly perceiving non-Christians' attitudes and thinking.

Power evangelism cuts through much resistance that comes from ignorance or negative attitudes; that is, it moves people along the Engel Scale quickly, especially overcoming negative attitudes toward Christianity. By penetrating the inner heart and consciousness, God overcomes resistance with the supernatural, resistance that through rational means only would take a lifetime—if not more—to overcome.

There are two communication dynamics taking place in evangelism: the natural, as described on the Engel Scale, and the supernatural, as seen in power evangelism, by which people are accelerated through the evangelism process.

Power evangelism is not antirational. If people are going to be converted, they need to know the essentials of the gospel, that they are sinners in need of God's grace and that grace is experienced through faith in Christ. But simply telling nonbelievers about Christ does not necessarily mean they will believe in him. Demonstrating the gospel through the gifts of the Spirit supports our message, frequently making persuasive arguments unnecessary, so nonbelievers know God's love and power. So by being aware of both dynamics, providing information and power demonstration, we can most effectively move people through the Engel Scale.

The difference between power evangelism and programmatic evangelism is analogous to the difference between the impact of a forty-five-caliber bullet and buckshot. The bullet is designed to wreak havoc on a small target; when accurately aimed at the place of greatest vulnerability it is always deadly. In comparison, buckshot is usually less effective because it relies more on chance hits. Divine appointments are like the impacts of forty-five-caliber bullets: they hit the specific target with penetrating force.

Several years ago, when the Vineyard Christian Fellowship was meeting in a high-school gymnasium, a middle-aged couple out for a walk wandered into the meeting. They had seen parked cars outside the school and were curious about the gathering; they never suspected it was a church meeting. They knew virtually nothing about Christianity.

They found a seat in the back of the room (we had begun worship and were singing) and within two or three minutes began to cry. They did not even know what the meeting was about! They simply liked the music and felt the presence of God. For a reason they did not understand it made them cry. When I asked anyone who wanted to be saved to come forward, they responded, even though I had not presented any information about the gospel or what it meant to be saved.

When asked what they wanted by one of our staff, they answered that they did not know—they had come forward because they could not stop themselves. On hearing a simple presentation of the gospel, they committed themselves to Christ. Of course, with such little knowledge of the gospel they needed immediate follow-up and instruction.

God's timing and power overcame all reservations. Here we see the wooing power of God operating on a transrational plane. They were drawn not by a message but by a supernatural presence. The message had to be given to complete the process, but without the drawing work of the Holy Spirit, the couple would not have readily accepted it.

LAUNCHING POINTS

Scripture is full of illustrations of divine appointments. Probably the most familiar in the life of Christ is the story of the Samaritan woman at Jacob's well (John 4:4–30). After asking her for a drink of water, Jesus used water as a launching point to explain spiritual truths. As the dialogue continued it became apparent that the woman had little accurate knowledge about the true nature of God.

Then Jesus said, "You have had five husbands, and the man you now have is not your husband." With this statement, he caught her attention. "Sir, I can see that you are a prophet," she said. That is, she realized that Christ was a seer, someone who can see the unknown—in this case her secret sins. After that she did not resist what Christ was saying. The result was that she believed. Through her testimony a revival started in the Samaritan community. "Come, see a man who told me everything I ever did. Could this be the Christ?" Through this divine appointment the Samaritan woman moved from some knowledge of God to repentance, from sin and to faith in Christ—all in a matter of minutes!

Several years ago a colleague of mine, Blaine Cook, on a flight from New York to Los Angeles received a word from God that he was going to lead one of the flight attendants to Christ. An hour into the flight (it is a five-hour trip), Blaine went to the back of the plane and began to talk with her. During their conversation, the Holy Spirit gave Blaine five specific pieces of information regarding her: she had great fear of never getting married; she had just broken off a relationship with a man with whom she was living; she had a major conflict with her mother; she was afraid of a physical illness; and she was afflicted with specific ailments. These thoughts came to him in rapid succession, flashes of intuition that Blaine knew were from God. He told her what he knew.

She immediately began to cry and asked him how he knew these things. "I know someone," he replied, "who will never leave you or forsake you and will heal you of your sicknesses." He prayed over her. She was physically healed. She then prayed to become a Christian.

A year later he was about to catch a plane back to New York, and God told him that he would see the flight attendant again. When he boarded the plane, there she was. She told him how she had joined a church in Manhattan, had not suffered any symptoms from her illnesses since he prayed over her, and was engaged to marry a Christian. As was true for the Samaritan woman, the flight attendant's resistance was overcome by an experience with the supernatural—the divine appointment motivated her to listen to the claims of the gospel and believe.

PATHWAYS TO GOD

In Acts 8:26–40 we read of another divine appointment involving one of the disciples. Philip was told by an angel to go south of Jerusalem to Gaza. He was then directed to go up to the chariot of an Ethiopian eunuch, a court official of the queen of the Ethiopians. (There is a high probability that to obey the Lord took great courage on Philip's part, for it is likely that as a high official the eunuch would have been heavily guarded. To approach such a man without permission could have meant death.)

At the time the Ethiopian eunuch was reading Isaiah 53:7–8. On the Engel Scale, the eunuch was at the decision point (−2); he only needed knowledge about what to believe. In God's providence, Philip was sent to explain the next step to him. But for this to happen Philip had to be listening to God and obedient to his word. After the Ethiopian eunuch's baptism, Philip was supernaturally transported away. To this day the eunuch is honored as the founder of the Ethiopian church. The harvest was ripe, but a willing worker was needed.

Frequently God arranges divine appointments for people with significant personal problems. We should not be surprised at this. At the beginning of his ministry, at the temple in Nazareth, Jesus proclaimed his mission was to "preach good news to the poor . . . freedom for the prisoners and recovery of sight for the blind, to release the oppressed, to proclaim the year of the Lord's favor" (Luke 4:18–19).

Difficult or dire human predicaments are pathways to bring people to salvation. By being more sensitive to the needs of those around us we frequently find situations in which we too can "proclaim the year of the Lord's favor."

The story of Jairus's daughter (Mark 5) is an excellent example of this. Jairus, a synagogue ruler, needed Jesus to heal his little daughter who was dying. While on the way to heal Jairus's daughter, Jesus was delayed when a woman who had been bleeding for twelve years touched him. She was healed. During this delay, news came that Jairus's daughter died. In response to the message, Jesus told Jairus, "Don't be afraid; just believe." On entering the home where the daughter lay, Jesus told those who were mourning that the child was only asleep.

They laughed at him, because they thought that he was ignorant of the facts. In first-century Middle Eastern society, everyone knew about life and death. The daily slaughter of animals for food or ritual observance made them familiar with death in a way that most modern people are not. Infant mortality was very high. Because of this, it was especially difficult for them to see Jairus's daughter as anything but dead.

As Jews they understood the resurrection of the dead to be a corporate event at the end of history, in the age to come. They did not expect an individual to be raised or that Jesus incarnated the resurrection. But the girl's death gave Christ an opportunity to demonstrate the kingdom of God, and in so doing the witnesses learned more about his true nature.

Many times we struggle with the same limitations as the Jews, the same inability to understand when God tells us to do something out of the ordinary—for example, to describe the personal illness of a stranger, as Blaine Cook did with the flight attendant. Most Christians miss out on exciting and powerful experiences in their lives either because they are not listening to God or, because of their inattentiveness, God is silent.

After putting the skeptics out of the house, Jesus took the parents and Peter, James, and John into the room with the girl. He then said, "Little girl, I say to you, get up!" The response of those present was astonishment; Jesus instructed them not to tell anyone about what happened. While not explicitly in the text, we may infer that Jairus and his household put their faith in Christ that day.

In October 1984 I witnessed a similar conversion in London. A pastor brought his father and mother to a conference at which I was speaking. His father was suffering from diabetes and blindness. During one of the meetings God told me that someone in the audience was blind and that the cause of the blindness was diabetes. In this instance I received a mental picture of the man's eye with the word diabetes coming to mind. (Sometimes I receive a pain in a part of my body that parallels the ailment in someone else God wants to heal. Other times I have a flash of intuition about someone. Over the years I have learned to recognize when these insights are from God and when they are a result of my imagination—or indigestion.)

I announced this to the gathering along with instruction that this person come forward to be healed by Jesus. (It was a large crowd; I had no prior knowledge of this man.) The father was healed. He received sight! As a result, many other family members (his mother, a nephew, brother, and others) encountered God's power. After the meetings their testimony was, "Now we know God in a way we never knew him before."

My point is not that they became Christians (they already had faith in Christ), but that their faith took on a new meaning and depth of commitment. This illustrates how we can move people along the Engel Scale even after their conversion; in this instance it was to the point of conceptual and behavioral growth (+3).

WHOLE HOUSEHOLDS

The goal of evangelism is not only the creation of individual disciples of Jesus; it also includes building bodies of people, the body of Christ. We have been created by God for fellowship. Right relationships are a part of God's plan for our lives. Because of this corporate or social dimension, we should not be surprised that God frequently brings clusters of people to his kingdom all at one time. Many times we are too focused on individuals, forgetting that when one member of a family or social grouping is affected, it can result in a whole family or town being won.

This was a common occurrence in the early church. As was true of the Philippian jailer and his household in Acts 16, we read of a royal official from Capernaum whose whole household was saved through power evangelism (John 4:46–53). He came seeking Jesus, asking him to heal his son. After rebuking the official for needing to "see miraculous signs and wonders" to believe, Jesus healed his son. What is unique about this miracle is that Jesus did not lay hands on the boy and pray over him. He simply declared the miracle done and told the official to go home. His son was healed. In response to the supernatural meeting of the official's need, "he and all his household believed."

Blaine Cook tells of a similar experience that he had in 1984 at a Baptist Church in a city in the Midwest. The pastor of this church of two hundred and fifty people had invited him to speak about healing. Many who attended were hostile to his message. During one of his talks Blaine said that he had a word of knowledge—he received a mental picture—regarding healing for a woman with an arthritic elbow. A member of the congregation, the daughter of a coal miner, was prayed for and healed. The next day this woman brought her daughter to be prayed over. The girl was born hydrocephalitic—she suffered from fourteen neurological conditions, including spina bifida. She was healed instantly of a wandering eye, bedwetting, and an open spine.

Her father, an elder in the church who until then had refused to come to the meetings, came the following day. He was closed to God acting here and now in the way that Blaine taught and was particularly antagonistic toward charismatic gifts. Though at first very hostile to Blaine's teaching, he relented and came because of what had happened to his wife and daughter. He could not deny the physical changes. During the meeting he for the first time put his full trust in Christ.

Before the meetings ended, most of the church was affected by what happened to the family; even many elders grew in their understanding of the kingdom of God and acceptance of the supernatural. In a few cases, elders admitted that they had been living more of a superficial Christianity than a true heartfelt faith. In the case of "spiritual leaders" in need of true, heartfelt conversion (a crossing of the Engel Scale's −1 point, repentance and faith in Christ), usually only encounters with the supernatural break through barriers of pride, religious hypocrisy, and spiritual blindness.

OUR PART FIRST

In divine appointments and the meeting of human needs the burden of responsibility for mediating the kingdom of God rests on Christians. Through obedient and teachable individuals God is able to perform signs and wonders, thus moving people along the Engel Scale more quickly than normally happens in programmatic evangelism.

Not only individuals and families, but whole towns are converted when God's power is released on hearts and minds. The villages of Lydda and Sharon were converted when Aeneas, a paralytic who had been bedridden for eight years, was instantly healed by Peter. As was true of Jesus, Peter used a simple and direct style in praying over Aeneas: "Jesus Christ heals you. Get up and take care of your mat" (Acts 9:34). Unlike Jesus, however, Peter did not heal in his own authority; Christ was the healer.

The evangelistic task was made easy for Peter because of Aeneas's healing. Most people respond positively to acts of mercy and demonstrations of spiritual power.

A certain attitude is required to keep divine appointments, one that permeated Jesus' and Peter's lives: how can God use me? Our part, as Jesus taught the Pharisees when they asked him about the greatest commandment, is to "love the Lord your God with all your heart and with all your soul and with all your mind" (Matt. 22:37). Divine appointments are occasions in which God chooses to do his works through our obedience, faith, hope, and love. They are *his* works, acts to which we add nothing.

This is a difficult attitude for Western Christians to attain, because we are trained to think that only the material is real, that the supernatural is fantasy. The reasons why and how to overcome them are the topics of the next chapter.

5. Signs and Wonders and Worldviews

Shortly after World War II, sociologists went to the Far East to investigate Asians' attitudes and thinking processes to see how they differed from the West's. They interviewed several thousand people and received surprising responses to questions based on syllogisms—in logic, a syllogism is a formal scheme of deductive reasoning. A typical question was: "Cotton doesn't grow in cold-weather countries. England is a cold-weather country. Does cotton grow in England?" The majority of Asians who answered the question said that they were not qualified to answer because they hadn't been to England.

In Western nations, even most third-grade children would have responded, "No. Cotton cannot grow in England. It is too cold." From earliest childhood, Western people are trained in deductive reasoning; we draw conclusions based on rules of logic to guide our lives. The presuppositions of our culture encourage us to think this way. The assumptions of most Eastern, African, and South American cultures do not—those cultures have more of an experiential base. The exception to this in those cultures is found among formally educated people. (I am not implying that our culture is superior to the others, only that it is different.)

The sociologists doing research in Asia discovered that Asians have a different way of understanding how the world works. Their worldview has heavy doses of animism, the belief that material objects possess a soul or spirit. They believe that spirits determine events, and because spirits are fickle and unpredictable, deductive reasoning does not help in knowing what might occur. Asians were not comfortable predicting whether cotton would grow in England even if they were told climatic conditions were right.

Author James Sire defines worldview as "a set of presuppositions (or assumptions) that we hold (consciously or subconsciously) about the basic makeup of our world."[1] Most of us are not conscious of our worldview. We do not learn it so much as absorb it from our surrounding culture. It is passed on from generation to generation with minimal change, the assumptions rarely being reviewed or revised. We assume that the way we understand life is how everybody does (or should), that our understanding of the world is reality.

Every culture has presuppositions, some conscious and many unconscious. We acquire paradigms—thinking patterns with which we evaluate our experiences—from parents, the media, art, education, and so on. Our worldview is like a lens—it colors, clarifies, classifies, warps, or partially excludes the world. It is, in Charles Kraft's words, our "control box" of reality.[2]

CULTURAL COHESIVENESS

Dr. Kraft, in his book *Christianity and Culture*, gives a more comprehensive definition of worldview:

Cultures pattern perceptions of reality into conceptualizations of what reality can or should be, what is to be regarded as actual, probable, possible, and impossible. . . . The worldview is the central systematization of conceptions of reality to which the members of the culture assent (largely unconsciously) and from which stems their value system. The worldview lies at the very heart of the culture, touching, interfacing with, and strongly influencing every aspect of culture.[3]

A worldview is necessary in the formation and maintenance of a culture. As Christians, our goal is not to shed entirely the worldview of whatever culture we might live in. Instead, our goal is to become conscious of our worldview and alter it to exclude values that are contrary to Christianity. Dr. Kraft points out four functions of a worldview.

A worldview provides an *explanation* of how and why things are as they are and how and why they continue or change. These explanations are passed on from generation to generation through folklore, myth, and stories. They also give the culture structure, a subsconscious legitimacy in the minds of the people.

A worldview serves as a basis for *evaluation*, for judging and validating experience. It is a yardstick with which people measure events and circumstances in the culture; it provides the criteria of acceptability.

For example, we find in the United States a worldview in which personal influence and material affluence are very important to life. This results in equating success with visible influence and material affluence. This worldview affects American Christians too. They might reject conspicuous material consumption and status-seeking life-styles, but frequently their way of judging "successful" churches nevertheless reflects the general culture's worldview: large congregations with big budgets are successful. When the Vineyard Christian Fellowship was a small, struggling—and controversial—church, I was shunned by many former colleagues and friends. Then we began to draw large numbers of people. Suddenly the Vineyard Christian Fellowship became a legitimate institution, acceptable in their eyes even though our so-called controversial teachings and practices had not changed. We had met their criteria for success: a large and growing membership and budget.

A worldview provides *psychological reinforcement* for a society's way of life. It creates a "we-they" dynamic: through a common worldview people identify with their society and see it as separate and distinct from all other societies. By accepting and living out the culture's worldview, one senses belonging to the larger group. This provides a sense of safety from fear of foreign values that might disrupt family, occupation, or religion. It also creates an environment in which relationships can grow—people are fairly confident that their neighbors see the world as they do, so they freely interact. A sense of community and membership in the clan, tribe, or nation is a byproduct of this psychological reinforcement. As the worldview is continually reinforced, the community is strengthened. A worldview serves an *integrating function* for new information, values, philosophies, and experiences. Not all new experiences that violate a culture's worldview are rejected outright. Some alter the culture, eventually creating a change in worldview. In this respect, worldviews are always evolving. Worldviews that resist evolution isolate their people from the rest of the world, making their cultures difficult to penetrate. Islamic cultures are excellent examples of this; they are without question the cultures most resistant to new ideas and values, including the gospel. Christian missionaries find Islamic cultures very difficult to penetrate.

Premodern, less technological worldviews, such as those once found among American Indians or African tribal peoples, create highly penetrable but fragile cultures, which are radically altered when modern technological cultures move in on them. The invaders have a shattering impact, leaving serious social problems in their wake, as the history of the American Indian all too tragically illustrates.

Secularized Western worldviews create societies that are highly penetrable but resistant to change in their overall makeup. Ideas from or portions of non-Western worldviews (for example, those found in Hindu, Islamic, or Communist societies) easily penetrate Western culture, but soon the alien views are blunted, absorbed, digested, transformed—usually losing their vitality and ability to profoundly influence the society. This absorbing, digesting, and blunting process also affects Christian ideas and values, tacitly secularizing the faith.[4]

THE WESTERN WORLDVIEW

Harry Blamires in his book *The Christian Mind* describes the dominant element of the modern Western worldview as secularism. "To think secularly," he writes, "is to think within a frame of reference bounded by the limits of our life on earth: it is to keep one's calculations rooted in this-worldly criteria."[5] The assumption of secular minds is that we live in a universe closed off from divine intervention, in which truth is arrived at through empirical means and rational thought.

Inherent in the modern Western worldview is a desire to control everything—people, things, events, even future events. The fifteenth-century Renaissance and then later the Reformation created an appetite in men and women to know more about nature. In swinging away from the medieval resignation of accepting all experiences as God's will, Western society eventually swung to the other extreme during the Enlightenment, making the human the measure of all things. By the nineteenth century materialism was entrenched in the Western worldview.

Materialism assumes that nothing exists except matter and its movement and modifications. For a materialist, only what can be seen, tested, and proved is real. The scientific method is elevated to Holy Writ. Working from this presupposition, Western people have learned to observe regularities and patterns in the material world and have developed a series of laws and principles for almost all areas of life: medicine, physics, philosophy, psychology, economics, and so on. These principles are thought of as consistent, stable, and dependable.

Christians cannot hold a philosophy of materialism and retain a Christian worldview. Materialism warps our thinking, softening convictions about the supernatural world of angels and demons, heaven and hell, Christ and Antichrist. We often live as though the material world is more real than the spiritual, as though material cause and effect explains all of what happens to us.

Rationalism seeks a rational explanation for all
making reason the chief guide in all matters of li
angels, demons, God, and spiritual gifts like
prophecy cannot be scientifically measured, secula
rationalism to explain away the supernatural. The main reason
secularists reject the supernatural is not that they believe in
cause and effect, though; it is because they exclude from reality
all phenomena that cannot be measured scientifically.

But twentieth-century rationalism is not necessarily an attempt to be rigorously rational. We must differentiate twentieth-century rationalism from the rationalism of the
Enlightenment in the eighteenth century. During the Enlightenment many materialists thought it was possible to rationally
analyze all experience and arrive at objective truth even in
areas like morality. Modern rationalists no longer believe this
is possible. In fact, there are many rational inconsistencies in
the way secularists think. For example, while believing in a
closed material universe that may be understood only by scientific inquiry, at the same time they hold relativistic assumptions about religion and morality. Believing that "whatever you
believe is okay for you" assumes a plurality of moral systems.
In this regard most secularists hold an internally inconsistent
worldview.

This accounts for the current growth in many Western societies of philosophies developed from areas of Eastern thought
like EST and Transcendental Meditation. On the surface interest in these philosophies seems to contradict what one would
expect from a materialistic worldview, but most modern secularists are not rigorously rational—they frequently ackowledge
there is a spiritual or moral world that lies outside the rational
and can only be known through personal experience. This
world cries for attention, but in the final analysis, materialism
and rationalism are incapable of satisfying it, of providing
plausible explanations for meaning in life. The secular worldview fails to satisfy people's need to understand the universe,
so they look for that meaning in philosophies and religions
that concern themselves with what lies outside the rational.

The experiences of Christian signs and wonders are *transrational*, but they serve a rational purpose: to authenticate the gospel. The gospel is opposed to the pluralistic lie that says all religious experience is equally valid. Signs and wonders validate Christ's lordship over every area of our lives, a relationship that can be described and understood.

CHRISTIAN WORLDVIEW

"To think Christianly," writes Harry Blamires, a former student of C. S. Lewis, "is to accept all things with the mind as related, directly or indirectly, to man's eternal destiny as the redeemed and chosen child of God."[6] For Blamires, thinking Christianly is equated with holding a Christian worldview. In his book *The Christian Mind*, Blamires mentions several elements in a Christian worldview.

"A prime mark of the Christian mind is that *it cultivates the eternal perspective*. . . . It is supernaturally oriented, and brings to bear upon earthly considerations the fact of Heaven and the fact of Hell."[7] This presupposition means that Christians believe in an open universe, a world in which God freely speaks and acts. This sets Christians in direct conflict with Western materialists, who operate on the basis that this world is all there is to life.

"The Christian mind has an *acute and sensitive awareness of the power and spread of evil upon the human race*."[8] Evil—the world, the flesh, and the devil—is constantly assaulting God's people. This awareness of evil means that Christians see themselves as members of an army, living in an alien land, locked in combat with Satan. There really is sin. There are evil spirits lurking about in the world. This awareness of evil also motivates Christians to rely on the Holy Spirit to overcome the Evil One.

"The *conception of truth* proper to the Christian mind is determined by the supernatural orientation of the Christian mind. . . . Truth is supernaturally grounded: it is not manufactured within nature."[9] In this regard, all experience is judged by God's revelation, whereas for the secularist truth is judged by the subjective self. For Christians, then, there is objective truth, rational propositions about God, the creation, and morality that can be known and are eternal. We believe in transcendent moral standards to which we can submit every aspect of our thinking.

Other elements that Blamires mentions are Christians' acceptance of God's authority and a high sense of the value of human persons.

At every one of these points, the Christian worldview is in conflict with the secular mind. Yet many Western Christians are unaware of the conflict, because in large part they have been secularized. A way of understanding how far many Christians' thinking is from God's ideals is by comparing the twentieth-century church with the first-century church. Jack Rogers in his book *Confessions of a Conservative Evangelical* gives some general characteristics of the Bible from which we can derive aspects of the worldview of those living at the time it was written. A comparison of these aspects with our current values is illuminating.

Scripture values the contemplative life. This is a result of holding a worldview that includes the supernatural. Because a biblical worldview rejects materialism, therefore meditation on eternal truths, God's Word, is of high value. An example of this is Psalm 77:6, where the psalmist "remembered [his] songs in the night" and "[his] heart mused and [his] spirit inquired" of God. Modern technological society, so concerned with time ("time is money"), has little patience for activity that has no apparent material benefit, that is rooted outside of time. (Perhaps this is one reason most Western Christians struggle with personal prayer.)

Scripture is poetic. This value comes from the Christian's understanding of revelation as being rooted in the supernatural, testifying to a reality beyond the temporal order. Intrinsic to this transcendent reality is beauty. So anything worth saying is worth saying beautifully. For example, Psalm 1 is a poetic picture of a righteous man. Materialism places higher value on pragmatism, is more concerned with "Does it work?" than "Is it beautiful?"

The Bible employs vivid picture language. Because God actually speaks and affects the material world, descriptions of how he works convey eternal truth. First-century Semites did not argue from a premise to a conclusion; they were not controlled by rationalism. Instead, they painted a word picture, employing descriptions of concrete situations, relationships, and places to make a point. There was a mistrust (or inability to comprehend) theological truths through abstract reasoning; the opposite holds true in Western culture today.

The Bible frequently uses symbolic language. Concrete objects can symbolize theological truths. Scripture is loaded with metaphors, similes, and other figures of speech. Western Christians, on the other hand, tend to take literally what is frequently supposed to be taken figuratively.

Scripture accepts paradox easily. For example, Western Christians have always found it difficult to accept the paradoxical truths of God's sovereignty and human freedom. They are preoccupied with logical consistency, a concern that first-century Christians did not have. Yet both doctrines are found in Scripture, and their incompatibility was not a topic of concern in the early church. That worldview allowed for apparent contradiction when touching on the mysteries of God. The Western church, more concerned with theological precision, has produced thousands of books trying to reconcile the two.

Religion in the Bible is a way of life. Relativism allows many competing belief systems in a society, making it impossible to develop one set of conventions and traditions. Lacking transcendent moral standards, Western culture tends to be protean, changing its form with every new fad.

Christianity, rooted in God's revelation and a highly developed sense of membership in the body of Christ, sees Christian truth touching every area of a person's life. Because God's revelation never changes and touches every area of life,

Christians can with confidence build distinctly Christian social environments and life-styles.

But Western Christians have found it difficult to build distinctively Christian life-styles. Distilling Christian teaching down to a set of creeds and code of ethics, they are usually more concerned with personal conduct and assent to doctrine than with a Christian life-style. They hold more of a Christian ethic or practice, not a way of life; they are concerned with following the "Christian rules." But Christianity is much more than a list of beliefs to which we assent. Early Christians lived in Christian communities in which every aspect of life—work, play, family, relationships—reflected a Christian way of doing things.

Twentieth-century Islam is comprehensive in its application of religious teaching to daily life. Law, economics, education, and almost every other area of culture reflect Islamic teaching in nations like Iran and Saudi Arabia. In this respect, modern Islam is a better analogy for the way and extent in which Christian values affected a way of life among first-century Christians than is Western Christianity today.[10]

This list could be greatly expanded. Each of the above characteristics challenges a fundamental component of the Western worldview. The Christian's challenge is to alter his or her worldview where it works against these biblical characteristics. If we do not alter our worldview, we will misunderstand Scripture, missing what God is teaching about how he works in the world.

THE EXCLUDED MIDDLE

Every worldview has cultural blind spots, those areas of life that are simply not taken into consideration or not assumed to work. In animist cultures (animism is the belief that all objects in the material world are inhabited by souls or spirits), the cause of smallpox is often assumed to be evil spirits. When modern medicine, which has largely eradicated smallpox in societies that receive smallpox vaccinations, has gone into these cultures to offer a cure in the form of vaccinations, it has often been refused, resulting in untold death and misery. The people were refusing something they thought could not possibly work against the evil spirits they thought were causing the illness.

The Western worldview has the opposite problem. Because secularists believe in a closed universe of material cause and effect, they cannot accept supernatural intervention. Christians who are influenced by this aspect of the Western worldview find healing of an illness when the cause for it is an evil spirit difficult to understand or accept.

Dr. Paul Hiebert, a professor in the Fuller Seminary School of World Mission, had this blind spot when he first went on the mission field:

John's disciples ask, "Are you he the one who was to come, or should we expect someone else?" (Luke 7:20). Jesus answered not with logical proofs, but by a demonstration of power in the curing of the sick and casting out of evil spirits. So much is clear. Yet when I read the passage as a missionary in India, and sought to apply it to missions in our day, I had a strange uneasiness. As a Westerner, I was used to presenting Christ on the basis of rational arguments, not by evidences of his power in the lives of people who were sick, possessed, and destitute. In particular, *the confrontation with spirits that appeared so natural a part of Christ's ministry belonged in my mind to a separate world of the miraculous—far from ordinary everyday experience* [emphasis mine].

Dr. Hiebert's "strange uneasiness" was soon tested by a smallpox plague in the village. He writes:

Doctors trained with Western medicine had tried to halt the smallpox but had not succeeded. The village elders finally sent for a diviner who told them that Maisamma, the Goddess of Smallpox, was angry at the village. To satisfy her and stop the plague, the villagers would have to perform a water buffalo sacrifice. The elders had to collect money to buy the water buffalo. The Christians refused to give any money. The elders got angry and forbade them to draw water from the wells and made the merchants refuse to sell them food. One of the elders of the Church in that village had come to get me at the mission station to pray for the healing of one of the Christian girls who was sick with smallpox. As I knelt, my mind was in turmoil. I had learned to pray as a child, studied prayer in seminary, preached it as a pastor. But now I was to pray for a sick child as all the village watched to see if the Christian God could heal.

He then poses the question: "Why my uneasiness both with reading the scripture and in the Indian village? Was the problem, at least in part, due to my own worldview—to the assumptions I as a Westerner made about the nature of reality and the way I viewed the world?" He then answers his own question:

People in the Indian villages have many diseases, curses of barrenness on women, bad tempers, bad luck, being possessed by spirits, and black magic practices. The Indian villagers have traditional ways of dealing with diseases:

1. Serious life threatening cases: With these cases they take the person to a *sadhu*—a "saint." This is a person of the gods who claims to heal by prayer. Because god knows everything they ask no questions. Because they are spiritual they charge no fees. But one is expected to give if a cure comes about.

2. Supernatural cases: With these cases they go to a *Mantrakar*—a "magician." This one curses by knowledge and control of supernatural forces and spirits, believed to be here on earth. They work with chants and visual symbols to control the forces and spirits. They ask no questions, receive no fees.

3. Medicine: Some people would go to doctors who cure by means of scientific knowledge based on medicine. They ask no questions but diagnose by feeling wrists, stomachs, etc. They charge high fees and give a guarantee that one only pays if the patient is healed.

4. Quacks: These people heal with folk remedies. They ask questions, charge low fees, give no guarantees. The people being treated have to pay before receiving treatment. (At the beginning, Western doctors were often equated with quacks.)

When a[n Indian] person became a Christian, he substituted the missionary for the saint! Christ replaced Krishna or Siva as the healer of their spiritual diseases. For the illnesses they had, they went to Western doctors or village quacks. But what about the plagues that the magician cured? What about spirit possession, or curses, or witchcraft, or black magic? What was the Christian answer to these?

Because of the Western culture's assumptions, the only conclusion one had was "They do not exist!" But to the people who really experienced these phenomena, there had to be an answer. So even the Christians turned to the magician for cures.[11]

Upon further reflection on his missionary experience, Dr. Hiebert uncovered a blind spot in his worldview. To describe his blind spot, he developed a three-tiered model of his Western worldview. This chart summarizes his thinking:

TRANSCENDENT WORLD BEYOND OURS: *includes* –hells, heavens, other times, i.e., eternity –high god (African); Vishnu, Siva (Hindu) –cosmic forces; karma –Jehovah, angels, demons, spirits of worlds	RELIGION faith sacred miracles otherworldly problems
SUPERNATURAL FORCES ON THIS EARTH: *includes* –spirits, ghosts, ancestors, demons –earthly gods and goddesses who live within trees, rivers, hills, villages –supernatural forces: mana, planetary influences, evil eyes, power of magic, sorcery, witchcraft –Holy Spirit, angels, demons, *Signs and Wonders*, gifts of the Spirit	EXCLUDED MIDDLE by Westerners

EMPIRICAL WORLD OF OUR SENSES:
includes
–folk sciences to explain how things occur
–explanations based on empirical observations
  • person shoots an arrow into a deer — he attributes death to arrow
  • one cooks a meal — attributes "cooked meal" to fire under pot
–theories about natural world—
  • how to build a house; plant crops; sail canoe
–theories about human relationships—
  • how to raise children; treat spouse, etc.
	SCIENCE
	sight &
	experience
	natural order
	secular
	this-worldly
	problems

The key tier on this chart is the "excluded middle." By dividing the universe into two totally separate worlds, Dr. Hiebert excluded supernatural intervention in the material universe (many Westerners, including Christians, think the same way). Another way the chart could be drawn, one that highlights our exclusion of the supernatural, is to make a thick, impenetrable line between the upper and lower tiers:

TRANSCENDENT WORLD BEYOND OURS: *includes* –hells, heavens, other times, i.e., eternity –high god (African); Vishnu, Siva (Hindu) –cosmic forces; karma –Jehovah, angels, demons, spirits of worlds	**RELIGION** faith sacred miracles otherworldly problems
EMPIRICAL WORLD OF OUR SENSES: *includes* –folk sciences to explain how things occur –explanations based on empirical observations • person shoots an arrow into a deer — he attributes death to arrow • one cooks a meal — attributes "cooked meal" to fire under pot –theories about natural world— • how to build a house; plant crops; sail canoe –theories about human relationships— • how to raise children; treat spouse, etc.	**SCIENCE** sight & experience natural order secular this-worldly problems

Animistic and most Eastern religions obliterate the barrier between the transcendent and empirical tiers. This confuses the spiritual and material worlds, resulting in frequently ascribing spiritual causes to physical problems. Using the adapted Hiebert chart, the animist's world looks like this:

TRANSCENDENT WORLD BEYOND OURS: *includes* –hells, heavens, other times, i.e., eternity –high god (African); Vishnu, Siva (Hindu) –cosmic forces; karma –Jehovah, angels, demons, spirits of worlds	**RELIGION** faith sacred miracles otherworldly problems
SUPERNATURAL FORCES ON THIS EARTH: *includes* –spirits, ghosts, ancestors, demons –earthly gods and goddesses who live within trees, rivers, hills, villages –supernatural forces: mana, planetary influences, evil eyes, power of magic, sorcery, witchcraft –Holy Spirit, angels, demons, *Signs and Wonders*, gifts of the Spirit	**EXCLUDED MIDDLE** by Westerners
EMPIRICAL WORLD OF OUR SENSES: *includes* –folk sciences to explain how things occur –explanations based on empirical observations • person shoots an arrow into a deer — he attributes death to arrow • one cooks a meal — attributes "cooked meal" to fire under pot –theories about natural world— • how to build a house; plant crops; sail canoe –theories about human relationships— • how to raise children; treat spouse, etc.	**SCIENCE** sight & experience natural order secular this-worldly problems

Of course, the world does not divide neatly into two groups of people, primitive animists and rationalistic materialists. There are many variations between these two extremes. For example, people who do not believe there is a transcendent reality—modern atheists, for example—would deny there is an upper tier.

The biblical worldview opens but does not obliterate the barrier between the lower and upper tiers. Completely removing the barrier leads to pantheism (equating God with the creation). The Christian worldview makes room for mystery in the relationship between the spiritual and material worlds. For example, the Christian worldview sees some illnesses as caused directly by demons and other illnesses as having physical causes.

Instead of being forced to the extremes of empiricism or animism, Christians see the *possibility though not the necessity* for supernatural intervention in all earthly experience. Again adapting the Hiebert model, the Christian worldview would look like this:

TRANSCENDENT WORLD BEYOND OURS: *includes* –hells, heavens, other times, i.e., eternity –high god (African); Vishnu, Siva (Hindu) –cosmic forces; karma –Jehovah, angels, demons, spirits of worlds	**RELIGION** faith sacred miracles otherworldly problems
SUPERNATURAL FORCES ON THIS EARTH: *includes* –spirits, ghosts, ancestors, demons –earthly gods and goddesses who live within trees, rivers, hills, villages –supernatural forces: mana, planetary influences, evil eyes, power of magic, sorcery, witchcraft –Holy Spirit, angels, demons, *Signs and Wonders*, gifts of the Spirit	**EXCLUDED MIDDLE** by Westerners
EMPIRICAL WORLD OF OUR SENSES: *includes* –folk sciences to explain how things occur –explanations based on empirical observations • person shoots an arrow into a deer — he attributes death to arrow • one cooks a meal — attributes "cooked meal" to fire under pot –theories about natural world— • how to build a house; plant crops; sail canoe –theories about human relationships— • how to raise children; treat spouse, etc.	**SCIENCE** sight & experience natural order secular this-worldly problems

Many Christians either exclude the supernatural from their worldview or consign it to the transcendent tier, where it can have no effect in their lives; by doing so they exclude God's power from their theology and its practice. Resisting what they cannot fully control or always understand, they miss out on doing Christ's works today.

LEARNING TO SEE

Worldviews exert a powerful influence on the minds of people and few are conscious of just how strong and controlling an influence it is. But human beings are not robots incapable of changing their programming. A group's worldview does not completely determine the perceptions of its individual members or subgroupings at all times. We interact with contrary worldviews as there is opportunity—through travel, reading, new relationships, and contact with the worldviews of other subgroupings within society or other societies.

Many evangelicals sincerely think that only Scripture study forms their thinking on such issues as healing or power evangelism. They are unaware of how powerful the influences of a Western, materialistic worldview are, how that worldview affects their perception of the supernatural in Scripture. Dr. Hiebert described this effect as a "strange uneasiness" when asked to pray for the sick girl.

Western Christians must undergo a shift in perception to become involved in a signs and wonders ministry, a shift toward a worldview that makes room for God's miraculous intervention. It is not that we allow God's intervention: he does not need our permission. The shift is that we begin to *see* his miraculous works and *allow* them to affect our lives.

Our ability to see and understand different phenomena is learned. Sometimes, because we have a different view of something or because we have not learned what to look for, we cannot see what is obvious to others. An analogy can be drawn from viewing the drawing opposite:

Do you see a young woman or an old hag? Some see a young woman, then, looking at the picture differently, an old hag. Others only see one or the other until someone shows them how to see the image differently. The lines of the drawing do not shift; the perception of the observer does. This, on a small scale, is analogous to a worldview change, a shift in perception.

It is difficult to recognize something you have not seen before. When you first see it, you do not comprehend it. Seeing in this respect is a learning process that takes place over a period of time.

So we do not see or notice everything we look at; we have selective perception. In the New Testament, dreams and visions are one of the means of communication that God uses in speaking to his people. They are even described as a normal part of the Christian life. Peter, quoting from Joel's prophecy, promised that the day had arrived when "your young men will see visions, your old men will dream dreams" (Acts 2:17). Yet how often do Western evangelicals today report dreams and visions? Is it because God is not revealing himself in this fashion or because a blind spot in our worldview prevents us from seeing what God is doing?

In many African tribal societies, dreams and visions are readily acknowledged and talked about among the people. Influenced by animism, they interpret such experiences from a spiritual, not psychological, perspective. When these people become Christians, they continue to attach spiritual signifi- cance to their dreams, only now they see them as coming from Jesus. (I am not implying here that all dreams are from Jesus, only that some may be and that these phenomena are common in Scripture.)

Many Third World missionaries on furlough attend my course on signs and wonders at Fuller Seminary. After I lecture on worldview, they usually comment to me on their inability to discuss supernatural phenomena when they are in the United States. Magic, sorcery, witchcraft—frequently seen on the mis- sion field—are viewed by many of the missionaries' American brothers and sisters as fantastic superstition, manifestations of "natives' " ignorance. If the missionaries describe these spiritual phenomena as real, they risk their credibility with financial supporters. So most missionaries remain silent.

Could it be that many Western evangelicals have subcon- sciously developed a theology that excludes the possibility of supernaturally inspired dreams and visions, harmonizing "Christian doctrine" with Western rationalism? This is not to question motives, only to note that worldview inhibits many evangelicals from seeing or accepting miracles.

I went through a process of learning to see the kingdom of God, of adjusting my worldview, as I began a signs and won- ders ministry. Jesus taught the disciples about spiritual eye- sight in response to their questions concerning the parable of the sower and the seeds in Matthew 13:11–16:

The knowledge of the secrets of the kingdom of heaven has been given to you, but not to them. . . . This is why I speak to them in parables:

Though seeing, they do not see;
 though hearing, they do not hear or understand.

In them is fulfilled the prophecy of Isaiah:

"You will be ever hearing but never understanding;
 you will be ever seeing but never perceiving.
For this people's heart has become calloused;
 they hardly hear with their ears,
 and they have closed their eyes.
Otherwise they might see with their eyes,
 hear with their ears,
 understand with their hearts, and turn, and I would heal them."

But blessed are your eyes because they see, and your ears because they hear.

This passage contains two principles about learning to see the kingdom of God. First, we need Christ's grace, his choosing to reveal to us the secrets of the kingdom. We can only see what God reveals to us. Because we live under the new covenant, the convenant of the Holy Spirit, we have confidence that God "will pour out [his] Spirit on all people" (Acts 2:17).

This leads to the second principle, which is how we receive kingdom grace. People with soft and teachable hearts openly receive and obey the words of the kingdom. The root problem for people not receiving the secrets of the kingdom is in the heart, in our motives and attitudes toward the things of God. But the passage goes on to say that there is a direct relationship between persons' hearts and their worldviews. A "hard heart," closed to the supernatural, cannot see or hear the secrets of the kingdom.

There are two ways that a hard heart affects our worldview. A hard heart may incline us toward a worldview that excludes the supernatural or it may prevent us from altering a faulty worldview to include the supernatural. In either case, the key to seeing the kingdom of God and doing the works of Christ is opening our hearts more fully to his Spirit. "But the one who received the seed that fell on good soil [an open heart] is the man who hears the word and understands it. He produces a crop, yielding a hundred, sixty or thirty times what was sown" (Matt. 13:23).

EXPECTATIONS

We see according to our expectations. Many times our expectations come from conditioning: we are taught to expect certain things in the Christian life and we miss what God is doing if he acts outside of our expectations. In Scripture, the story of the feeding of the multitude illustrates how prior conditioning blinds us to learning about the kingdom of God. After Jesus fed thousands, the people said, "Surely this is the Prophet who is to come into the world" (John 6:14). Jesus withdrew from there because "they intended to come and make him king by force." Because the Jews assumed that the Messiah was coming in part to reestablish a political kingdom like David's, whenever they saw Jesus perform a miracle and identified him as the Messiah, they thought he had come to establish his political kingdom. Even the disciples, after the resurrection, worked under this assumption (see Acts 1:6). They had the *expectation* of an earthly king.

Years ago I was embarrassed by people in my church who talked about strange, supernatural experiences. Once a woman came to me and described her conversion experience. (She had tried to talk with another pastor about it, but he refused to listen.) She did not fully understand what happened to her and needed help from a pastoral leader. One evening she came home from a party and on entering her house sensed the presence of someone. It frightened her, but she could not find anyone. Later, in her bedroom, she heard a voice. All it said was "Rosa Lee." Her friends knew her only as Lee, even though her full name was Rosa Lee. She turned and saw no one. Then she heard the voice again. This time she asked,

"Who is it? Lord?" "Yes, Rosa Lee. It is time for you to know me." She fell on her face and received Christ as her Savior. When she told me her story, I thought that she was very strange, if not slightly demented. Hearing voices? I took her through the biblical steps to salvation to ensure that she was *really* saved. She left our meeting hurt. My worldview, my expectations about how God speaks to people today, controlled how I interpreted her experience, and as a result I cheapened her conversion experience. (I thank God that years later, after growing in my understanding of the supernatural, I met her again and apologized for what I had done. She graciously forgave me.)

Our expectations are affected by our worldview, our assumptions about the nature of reality. These assumptions also affect communication, especially our ability to understand language. Sometimes only slight deviations in how we perceive the world make great differences. In John 2:13–22 we read of Jesus taking a whip of cords to businessmen in the Temple courts. The Jews asked, "What miraculous sign can you show us to prove your authority to do all this?" They were asking for proof that he was the Anointed One. This is not a surprising question, for the Jews were at the Temple, indicating their devotion and knowledge of Scripture. They believed in the supernatural. Jesus answered, "Destroy this temple, and I will raise it again in three days." Jesus was speaking of his physical body but the Jews assumed Jesus was speaking about the Temple building in Jerusalem. They could not understand what Jesus was saying, because, though holding a similar worldview to Jesus, there was a crucial theological difference between the two. The Jews could not accept the incarnation. Their theological presuppositions, especially a concern to avoid scrupulously polytheism, precluded their hearing Christ's messianic claims. (Lurking beneath the surface of their theological problem, I suspect, were hard hearts.)

The Jews held a set of assumptions about the Temple: it was where God was supposed to dwell, a place built out of stone where they were standing. Based on their knowledge about the Temple, their conclusion that Christ was referring to the Temple building was reasonable. Of what other temple could Jesus have been speaking? But their knowledge was incomplete, forcing them to draw wrong conclusions. They missed learning a central truth about the kingdom of God: the Lamb of God must die for the sins of the world.

In this instance, Jesus was prophesying about his future death on the cross. He was alluding to the future event of the resurrection, a sign and the ultimate proof of his authority to clear the Temple courts. Only later, after the resurrection, did the disciples understand his words.

Further information and instruction coming at the crucifixion itself was the key to interpreting correctly Christ's response to the Jews. This further information altered their assumptions about the Temple and Jesus (that the house of God should not be a marketplace and that Jesus had the authority to clear it of any who were making it so). So correct interpretation was influenced by an experience—the experience at the cross in this instance. Evangelicals believe that experience should not determine theology, that experience must always be subordinated to Scripture. While I agree with this, I think there is a sense in which our experience legitimately adds to the interpretation process by altering assumptions, as was the case with Christ's statement to the Jews about the temple.

I have talked with many evangelical theologians who have undergone significant changes in their theology because of an experience. We are always being influenced by our experiences and need the humility to admit it. The question is: what are our criteria for judging these experiences? As we continue to experience Christian living and God, our thinking ought to become more and more scriptural. All too often, though, a secularized worldview filters experience, separating out anything that contradicts modern materialism.

There is another way in which our experience legitimately affects theology. Some truths in Scripture cannot be understood until we have had certain experiences. I have found this the case with healing. Until I began to experience people being healed, I did not understand many of the Scripture passages on healing.

The Bible frequently points us toward experiences that we have not already had, implying that as we have these experiences we will grow in biblical knowledge. Sacrificial love of Christian brothers and sisters and acts of mercy are like that; as we obey, light reflects from our good works back on Scripture, revealing more about God's grace and mercy.

So God uses our experiences to show us more fully what he teaches in Scripture, many times toppling or altering elements of *our* theology and worldview. This is what he accomplished with the disciples through their experience of his crucifixion and resurrection. Only then were they able to understand his earlier words at the Temple to the Jews: "Destroy this temple, and I will raise it again in three days."

THEOLOGY

All that I have said about worldviews points toward one conclusion: Christians' worldviews affect their theology. If Christians have a worldview that is affected by Western materialism, they will probably deny that signs and wonders are for today. Though they may use a theological rationale, the real issue is that it upsets their worldview. In contrast to this, a second group of Christians have a worldview that is affected by Western rationalism; they might acknowledge signs and wonders, but consign them to the irrational. These people seek signs and wonders for the thrill of the experience, as an end in itself. They do not understand the purpose of signs and wonders: to *demonstrate* the kingdom of God.

If we believe in a theology that does not include the possibility of contemporary Christians doing the works of Jesus— including signs and wonders—we will not have a practice of signs and wonders. Kevin Springer knows of a man whose wife was healed after her doctors told him she would not live through the night. The evening the doctors informed him that his wife was terminally ill, he called his church elders and asked them to come and pray for her. The elders were not convinced that God heals today but nevertheless came out of obligation. They prayed over her, anointing her with oil, and— to their surprise—the next day she walked out of the hospital. The doctors called it "a miracle." What is remarkable about this incident is that the elders never told the congregation what happened! They were not as elated as the doctors. Further, this miraculous event did not stimulate the practice of prayer for the sick in the church. Why? Because their theology placed a cloud over an obvious miracle, and they had not developed models for the practice of healing. Even if they openly acknowledged the healing, they would not know how to incorporate the healing ministry in the church. So God healed *in spite of* them; his mercy was greater than the elders' unbelief.

In the last chapter of Acts, we read that Paul was bitten by a viper on the island of Malta. The people from Malta responded first by thinking Paul was a murderer who escaped drowning in the sea but "Justice [had] not allowed him to live." The Maltese had a cosmic worldview: they assumed interaction between the cosmic and empirical worlds. First they interpreted the viper's bite as God's judgment. Then, seeing Paul alive, they assumed that Paul was a god. For them, only a god would not die from such a bite. The idea that God intervenes directly in the affairs of men and women was an unconscious presupposition.

Secularized people might have said, "It must have been an old snake" or "It bit someone earlier in the day and was low on poison." Western Christians often think the same way, perhaps adding, "God planned that an old snake would be there in order to save Paul." Our assumptions control our conclusions as much as the Maltese assumptions controlled theirs.[12]

6. The Works of Jesus

So far I have established three premises that are the basis for power evangelism. First, two kingdoms, the kingdom of God and the kingdom of Satan, are in conflict, and Christians have been drafted in Christ's army to do battle against Satan. Second, evangelism is meant to go forward in the power of the Holy Spirit. And third, our worldviews affect how we understand Scripture, including passages about signs and wonders.

Keeping these in mind, let us now examine in more detail what Christ did, especially his works of signs and wonders. Jesus' signs and wonders were his calling card, one of the proofs that the kingdom of God had come. Theologian Herman Ridderbos writes, "This factual relation between the coming of the kingdom and Jesus' miracles is brought out not only by the casting out of devils but also by Jesus' other miracles, for they all prove that Satan's power has been broken and that, therefore, the kingdom has come."[1] Jesus' miracles have another purpose: to show us what the kingdom of God is like, to reveal glimpses of God's love, peace, and joy.

CATEGORIES OF MIRACLES

C. Peter Wagner, in *Church Growth and the Whole Gospel*, outlines two categories of signs of the kingdom found in Scripture:[2]

Category A: Social signs, those applied to people in general:
    Preaching the good news to the poor
    Proclaiming release to the captive
    Liberating the oppressed

Instituting the Year of Jubilee

Category B: Personal signs, signs applied to specific individuals:

Restoring sight to the blind
Casting out demons and evil spirits
Healing sick people
Making the lame walk
Cleansing lepers
Restoring hearing to the deaf
Taking up poisonous serpents
Raising the dead
Speaking in tongues
Calming storms
Feeding thousands
Drinking deadly poison with no ill effect

Describing Category B, Wagner says:

It is what the Bible refers to when it records the prayers of the believers in Jerusalem, "Stretch out your head to heal and perform miraculous signs and wonders through the name of your holy servant Jesus" (Acts 4:30). . . . The main function of Category B signs is to draw attention to the power of God in order to open unsaved people's hearts to the message of the gospel."[3]

Miracles are a foreshadowing and promise of coming universal redemption and the fullness of the kingdom. Casting out demons signals God's invasion of the realm of Satan and Satan's final destruction (Matt. 12:29; Mark 3:27; Luke 11:21ff.; John 12:31; Rev. 20:1ff.). Healing the sick bears witness to the end of all suffering (Rev. 21:4). Miraculous provisions of food tell us about the end of all human need (Rev. 7:16ff.). Stilling storms points forward to the complete victory over the powers using nature to threaten the earth. Raising the dead announces that death will be forever done away with (1 Cor. 15:26).[4]

Jesus himself performed signs and wonders that demonstrated his reign over four areas by which Satan particularly works—demons, disease, destructive nature, and death. In each of the power encounters described below Jesus is doing the works of the Father.

DEMONS

In a June 1982 meeting of the Consultation on the Relationship Between Evangelism and Social Responsibility (sponsored by the World Evangelical Fellowship and the Lausanne Committee on World Evangelization), fifty evangelical leaders from twenty-seven different countries gathered in Grand Rapids, Michigan, to discuss social signs of the gospel. In their final report, we read:

We believe that signs should validate our evangelism. . . . The third sign of the kingdom was exorcism. We refuse to demythologize the teaching of Jesus and his apostles about demons. Although the "principalities and powers" [see Ephesians 6:12] may have a reference to demonic ideologies and structures, we believe that these certainly are evil personal intelligences under the command of the Devil. Demon possession is a real and terrible condition. Deliverance is possible only in a power encounter in which the name of Jesus is invoked and prevails.[5]

Jesus never met a demon that he liked, and he met them frequently. Demon expulsion is a direct attack by Jesus on Satan, a primary goal of Jesus' mission. "The reason the Son of God appeared," John writes in his first Letter, "was to destroy the devil's work" (1 John 3:8). James Dunn writes, "The binding of Satan was expected by the Jews as a mark of the close of the age."[6] In this regard Christ's worldview was similar to the Jews'. Jesus came to fulfill that expectation by destroying the works of the devil and his minions.

Satan's methods of attack vary: people are tempted or inflicted with physical and emotional hurt, their lives are threatened or they are possessed by demons. Demons exert various degrees of influence over people. In some cases, such as in demonic possession, they gain a high degree of control over the human will. In Scripture, demons cause dumbness (Matt. 9:32–33), physical blindness (Matt. 12:22–23), and epilepsy (Matt. 17:14–21). Mental insanity is suggested in Mark 5, where the healed Gerasene demoniac is described as clothed and in his right mind, suggesting that before he was not. Of course, not *all* (or even most) physical, emotional, and psychological problems are caused by Satan; however, in some instances they may be caused by him.

Jesus withstood Satan's attacks in the wilderness, then immediately taught that the rule of God was near (Mark 1:15). Soon after his wilderness temptation, during his first sermon (in the synagogue at Capernaum), Jesus cast out a demon from a man (Mark 1:21–28). Before being cast out, the demon inquired, "Have you come to destoy us?" This question reveals a knowledge of what God has in store for demons at the end of the age. Jesus, through his actions, demonstrated that he had come to destroy them, though that destruction will not be accomplished fully until the age to come.

Jesus told the demon to "be quiet" and "come out of him [the man]". The former phrase is frequently translated, "He rebuked him." It means to denounce or censure in order to end an action. What he said was "Stop it! That's enough!" "Be quiet" conveys the idea of strangling or muting. He throttled the demon, and the demon left. Jesus saw the man as a victim of an unseen force, and he dealt ruthlessly with the spirit.

The disciples also expelled demons. We also advance the kingdom of God in the same way: overthrowing every contrary spirit in the name of our King. Too many Christians do not know how to deal with demons. They are afraid of evil spirits. They do not understand the scriptural basis for our authority and power over them. We can and ought to treat evil spirits ruthlessly—binding, rebuking, and casting them out whenever we encounter them.

Authority over demons is power that Christ freely gives Christians. When the Seventy-two returned from their missions, they said, "Lord, even the demons submit to us in your name." Christ responded, "I saw Satan fall like lightning from heaven. I have given you authority to trample on snakes and scorpions and to overcome all the power of the enemy; nothing will harm you" (Luke 10:17–19). There is no doubt that we possess all the authority we need to overcome demons (Mark 16:17–18; Acts 1:8; Rev. 12:11). Jesus was acknowledging the battle that we have been thrown into on earth, that God had thrown Satan out of heaven, and that we need not fear his power to hurt.

In 1981 I spoke at a conference in the Anglican parish of St. Michael-le-Belfrey, York, England. During one of the meetings I was introduced to a woman in her early twenties who had been acting strangely in the back of the church. She was cowering like a frightened animal. (Later I learned that she suffered from serious metabolic disorders and an assortment of psychological problems, complicated by prolonged drug abuse. She was in constant physical and emotional pain.)

I bent over to look into her face. Her eyes were entirely rolled back, so I could see only the white parts and none of the pupils. There was a sensitivity, an uneasiness, in my own spirit that indicated this was probably more than an emotional problem. (I find this sensation difficult to describe because it is spiritual, not physical, in nature.) She spoke to me in a very gruff, masculine voice, blaspheming the Lord and me. The voice told me that Jesus Christ had no authority or power, and neither did I. The voice further said, "This woman is mine. You can't have her. Stay away." Based on these responses I assumed she was a fully demonized person.

I spoke to the demon who was temporarily in control of her conscious mind, and said, "I command you to release this girl." Immediately her eyes rolled back down and her voice and personality changed to that of a young woman.

She began weeping and said, "I'm frightened."

I responded, "I know. Do you want help?"

She said, "They say they will kill me if I ask for help."

I told her that they could not kill her at that point. "If you want help, there is help here."

"I do want help."

I told her to come with me, and immediately the demon tried to take over her personality again, attempting to force her withdrawal. I again commanded the demon to be silent.

We went through the crowd until we found pastor David Watson. I explained the situation to David, asking his permission to minister to her. He approved and asked if he too could pray for her. I agreed.

I took the girl, David Watson, and ten or twelve ministry team members into a small room of the church. Then I asked the manifesting demon its name and what it did to the girl. It told me its name and said it made her want drugs. We cast that demon out by name.

For seven hours the woman intermittently told her story and we prayed over her, taking authority over different types of demons as they identified themselves. Eventually we cast out some forty demons. During the interviews we learned that she had been in and out of state hospitals all of her life, had been molested since the age of six, and had serious involvement with the occult.

After this process she was able to repent of her sin and receive Christ as Lord and Savior. Her life was immediately changed. (A detailed report of this incident was written by David Watson and submitted to his bishop.)

In 1982 she came to Yorba Linda for three months and stayed in the home of one of our church members. She was no longer demonized, but she still had some social and emotional problems. She received counseling help in Yorba Linda and England and overcame most of these problems. In October of 1985 I was in Sheffield, England, and spent time with her. She had just graduated from the university and was beginning her student teaching. She brought with her a young man with serious demonic problems. A ministry team from the Vineyard ministered to him!

DISEASE

One of Satan's most effective tools is disease. Almost half of all the verses in the Gospels involve some form of power encounter, with healing accounting for from nine to twenty percent.[7] Yet too often we read these accounts through the filters of modern scientism, assuming physical disease has only a physical cause and solution. Subconsciously or consciously, we read of healings in the New Testament and assume that either they were only for the early church or there is another explanation—a scientific one—for how these healings actually occurred. For this reason, for years the only prayer for healing that I practiced was "Lord, guide the surgeon's hands." I still pray that sometimes, but I have many more options now.

Causes of disease may be physical, psychological, or spiritual. Regardless of the cause, though, Christians have power over disease. Christians in the first century saw disease as a work of Satan, a weapon of his demons, a way in which evil rules the world. When Jesus healed disease, whether demonically or physically caused, he pushed back the kingdom of Satan. What the devil did, Jesus undid.

In Luke 13:10–17 we read of a woman crippled for eighteen years who was healed by Jesus. Jesus called her forward and said, "Woman, you are set free from your infirmity." She had been incarcerated by Satan, and Jesus was setting the captive free. "Then he put his hands on her, and immediately she straightened up and praised God."

In response to attacks from the Pharisees (because Jesus healed her on the Sabbath, a day of rest for the Jews), Jesus said, "You hypocrites! . . . Should not this woman, a daughter of Abraham, *whom Satan has kept bound for eighteen long years*, be set free . . . ?" His was not a medical explanation. He identified the cause of her problem as Satan's doing. The Pharisees operated with hardness of heart and religious blindness.

They hid behind theology, in this case the prohibition of work on the Sabbath.

During Christ's time, Edward Langton asserts in his book *Essentials of Demonology*, "Special demons came to be associated with particular forms of disease or sickness. Certain diseases were held to be caused by particular demons."[8] Again, not *all* cases of disease are caused by demons or are demons. Often, of course, there are psychological or physical explanations for illness. But more frequently than many Western Christians realize, the cause is demonic.

Seeing demons as a possible cause of disease is difficult to accept, because it challenges modern, materialistic notions about disease and infirmity. In Jesus' day, his explanation "Satan has kept [her] bound" was accepted easily. Not even the Pharisees questioned it. Today, most Western people assume that her curvature of the spine was caused by an accident or developmental problem. Yet, whatever the means, Jesus thought Satan was the cause. We have been called to deal with the cause, not with how Satan inflicts disease and suffering.

Western Christians all too often look at disease and infirmity and accept it, saying, "It must be the will of God" or "We'll understand it better when we get to heaven." In some cases God *doesn't* heal. But frequently people make these statements to mean God doesn't *want* to heal anyone today. In this sense, these statements are platitudes, falling short of what God has for us. He is a God of mercy and love and has given us the authority to do the works of Jesus.

In 1981, while in Johannesburg, South Africa, I was asked to pray over a fourteen-year-old Zulu boy who had not grown an inch since age seven. His toes were partially missing; he suffered from a cleft palate and ruined teeth; he was incapable of speaking or walking (his mother carried him to the meeting). I was deeply saddened when I saw him.

When I spoke to him, he responded with incoherent mumblings. To get closer to him, I got down on my hands and knees. He looked up at me like a haunted animal—slobbering, mumbling, growling. His pupils rolled back in his head. He shrank back in terror when I spoke the name of Jesus. I knew then that I was dealing with a demon in him.

So I called over several other Christians, people who I knew were experienced in deliverance, and we began praying over the boy. While praying, Becky Cook, an associate, discerned that a curse was on him. (She knew this through a word of knowledge; she had no previous knowledge of the boy or his family.) Someone had called demons on him when he was younger, asking them to torment and kill the boy. It was not clear at that time who had spoken the curse, but it seemed to be the source of his problems. We broke the power of the curse by speaking against it in the name of Christ and then cast out several demons who were afflicting him.

Later we learned that when he was seven years old, living in another town, the boy had been a runner for a witch doctor, his aunt. His mother decided to move. Because the witch doctor was losing his service, she placed a curse on the child. The day the aunt placed the curse on the boy, the mother returned home to find him in a degenerated, animal-like condition. Over the years his condition had grown worse, until we encountered him in Johannesburg.

The results of breaking the curse were remarkable. Within two days, the boy returned to the meetings walking and able to recognize me. His mother reported that he had made remarkable progress since we prayed for him. We prayed for him again that day, without much more progress. After we left South Africa, other Christians followed up with regular prayer. Four months later, he returned home (he had been institutionalized). He enrolled in school and in several months advanced two grade levels.

In Luke we find the story of Peter's mother-in-law's healing (Luke 4:38–39). Jesus, Scripture reports, "Rebuked the fever." This is the same language that Jesus used to drive the demon out of the man in the synagogue at Capernaum. It might well be that the origin of the mother-in-law's fever was a demon.

She was healed instantly. Jesus frequently spoke the same way to fevers as he did to demons, because he saw the connection between sickness and Satan.

Another tool for healing is God's forgiveness. When the paralytic was lowered through the roof in Capernaum, Jesus said, "Son, your sins are forgiven" (Mark 2:5). In response to the Pharisees' attack on him for forgiving the paralytic's sins, Jesus asks, "Which is easier: to say, 'Your sins are forgiven,' or to say, 'Get up, take your mat and walk'?" He then healed the paralytic. Obviously forgiveness of sins is a far greater miracle, for it opens the door to eternal life—the goal and purpose for signs and wonders.

There is great power in forgiveness of sin. In 1984 I spoke at a conference in the Midwest. After one of the meetings, in the parking lot I met a woman who suffered with crippling arthritis. Her pain was so great that she needed a walker to get about. I talked with her before praying and discovered that her husband had abandoned her and her daughter fourteen years earlier, and it was shortly thereafter that her arthritic problems began. She also told me—and her daughter, who was with her—that her husband had run off with another man. She had kept this information from her daughter all these years.

On hearing this, I became enraged at what Satan had done and said, "That's enough!" Here was an instance when the Holy Spirit stirred my heart, showing me that the source of arthritis was her yielding to bitterness toward her husband and God. I was angered by what Satan had done, and so was the Holy Spirit.

When I spoke those two words (they almost exploded out of me), the power of God fell on the woman. Her body trembled violently; her fingers and legs seemed to be straightened. Satan's grip, the power of bitterness and accusation, was broken. Then she confessed her sin of harboring bitterness toward her husband and God. I reassured her of God's forgiveness. That night she was healed of about eighty percent of her condition.

More prayer was needed for the other twenty percent. Sin that finds safe harbor in our bodies is capable of all sorts of physical damage. Receiving and extending forgiveness was a key to her healing.

NATURE

Just as demonic forces cause havoc in the lives of men and women through sickness and demonization, they can also exert their perverted influence in nature by causing it to run amok. In the fourth chapter of Mark's gospel, Jesus wars on "a furious squall" and waves that threatened to swamp his and the disciples' boat as they crossed a lake. This story is often used to illustrate inward harmony for Christians as they encounter the various winds and waves of life's challenges. While this analogy may be a good one, it overlooks the primary intent of the author, which is to show Jesus ruling over nature itself.

Western materialists find Christ's rule over events in nature very difficult to accept. They see Christ's calming of the seas as a fantastic story smacking of animism and suggesting primitive religion, even superstition. The equating of *all* natural calamity with evil spirits would be animism, but simply acknowledging the possibility of Satan's influence in nature, and Christ's lordship over that influence, is not animism.

Christians also succumb to rationalism, thinking, "Well, that's Christ's divinity ruling over natural forces—it doesn't relate to how we live today." Yet the Bible teaches that Jesus performed miracles to demonstrate that he had the authority and power to do so, and that his power is available to us to do the same works.

The disciples in the boat were experienced fishermen. They knew the waters and what the storm could do; they thought that they were going to die. "Teacher," they said, "don't you care if we drown?" After calming the storm, Jesus rebuked them for being afraid and lacking faith. Jesus' response used to puzzle me. Was not their fear reasonable, considering the circumstances? Then one day, while I was sitting beside the Sea of Galilee and meditating on this passage, the opening words of the text came to mind: "He said to his disciples, 'Let us go over to the other side.' " The same person who said, "Let there be light" said, "Let us go over to the other side." When he asked, "Do you still have no faith?" it was because he had already declared that they were going to the other side. The sure knowledge of the Father's will gave Jesus the liberty to sleep soundly while crossing, even during a storm. The disciples had to awaken him!

The words that Jesus used to calm the lake, "Quiet. Be still." are similar to those used to overcome demons and disease. He saw in nature's attack the work of Satan. This was a classic power encounter in which Jesus was at war with the perpetrator of destruction.

When I first began teaching my church congregation about this type of power encounter I had a humorous (and humbling) experience. In May of 1982 I preached a series of sermons about the works of Jesus in nature. During the week between my third and fourth sermons I traveled to Denver, Colorado, where I had a speaking engagement.

Denver is called the "Mile-High City," so named for its location over five thousand feet up in the majestic Rocky Mountains. Sudden spring storms with accumulations of twenty or more inches of snow are not unusual. On Thursday one of these storms hit the city, shutting down the airport and slowing automobile traffic. I decided to pray against the storm. For two days I prayed and nothing happened. The storm intensified. I was trapped in Colorado for the weekend.

That Sunday morning back in sunny southern California, Bob Fulton, my copastor at the Vineyard Christian Fellowship, stood before the congregation and announced that I would not be preaching. "A storm has hemmed John in the Rocky Mountains," he said. "He won't be able to tell us about the authority of Christ over nature." I am told that it took several minutes before the laughter died down, and to this day church members occasionally remind me of the incident.

Not all stories of praying against storms end in failure. C. Peter Wagner reports a remarkable incident that occurred in September 1984 at a Stuttgart, Germany, meeting of the Lausanne Committee on World Evangelization. During the meetings the committee received reports that hurricane Diana was about to slam into the southeastern coast of the United States, with the state of North Carolina taking the main blow. The reports were alarming; it was estimated that there could be great loss of life and property. Leighton Ford, president of the Lausanne Committee on World Evangelization, owned a home in the anticipated path of the storm. He thought that he and many others could easily lose their homes.

"It was about 10:30 in the morning when we received word of Diana," Dr. Wagner now recalls. "Right there, in the meeting, Kristy Mosvold of Norway suggested that I pray against it. So I stood up and began to pray, using the pattern of Christ's prayers against storms. Under what I felt as a special anointing of the Spirit I took authority over it, rebuking it." Two hours later the committee received word on the Armed Services Network that the hurricane had mysteriously stalled out at sea. Leighton Ford's home was spared. The next week *Newsweek* magazine ran an article in which meterologists said Diana's sudden turn away from the coast was inexplicable. Later Diana returned and struck a glancing blow at the coast, but damage was minimal and nothing happened inland.

Perhaps what happened was a quirk of nature, the explanation for which modern scientists do not yet have the technology to discern. But, based on Scripture, another plausible explanation is that God answered the Lausanne Committee's prayers, preventing the loss of many homes and lives and sparing much suffering.

DEATH

"The end will come," taught Paul, "when [Jesus] hands over the kingdom to God the Father after he has destroyed all dominion, authority and power. For he must reign until he has put all his enemies under his feet. *The last enemy to be destroyed is death"* (1 Cor. 15:24–26). Jesus hated death—Satan's most fearful weapon—because it is final.

Unlike delivering people from evil spirits, which Christ appeared to do every time he encountered a willing person, and healing, which he did with great frequency, resuscitation was infrequent. But the miracles of resuscitation—restoration to life of deceased persons—have enormous significance. Perhaps more than any other kind of miracle, they were a foretaste of the age to come, clear signals to Satan that his world was being invaded and overpowered by Jesus. The Gospels record three specific and one general account of his raising the dead.[9] These miracles strike Satan at his greatest point of strength and signal that his reign was broken by Jesus.

In Luke 7 Jesus raised from the dead a widow's son. Coming to the town of Nain, he encountered the widow's son's funeral procession. Luke wrote, "When the Lord saw her, his heart went out to her and he said, 'Don't cry.' " He then commanded her son to get up. The crowd's response was to exclaim that "God has come to help his people."

Jesus is the embodiment of his Father, of the same nature, functioning in perfect concert with his will for the redemption of the human race. The Father's will is to help people, to extend compassion and mercy. Resuscitation assured the people that God loved them, and that some day even death would be overcome.

The idea that Christ could raise someone from the dead *today* is difficult for many Western Christians to accept. Yet I have heard many reports (most from non-Western countries) of God working in this way. Believing in the *possibility* of someone being raised from the dead today has an impact on modern Christians' faith and practice.

During the summer of 1981, Bill Pahl, a member of the Whittier, California, Vineyard Christian Fellowship, went on a weekend retreat in the majestic Sierra Nevada mountains. "There were about ten people in our little expedition—all members of a small group from my church," Bill recalled. "One morning we went into the woods and discovered a beautiful cascade, fifteen feet wide, hidden in a lush ravine. The rocks all about were worn from decades of water rushing over their once jagged surfaces, polishing and covering them with a microscopic algae coating that made a treacherous crossing.

"As I walked across the stream at the base of the cascade I lost my footing, going head over heels, the back of my head hitting squarely on an outcropped rock."

Lying in the water, Bill knew he was seriously hurt. "I felt my life ebb as I slipped in and out of consciousness. The others rushed to my aid, pulling me from the stream, then fervently praying. They thought I was dead. Later I found out that for three minutes I had no signs of life.

"Our pastor, John McClure, had been teaching about the power of God over death. By praying over me to live, members of my small group were acting on what they had been taught and come to believe—that God can raise people from the dead even today.

"It is hard to describe what went on inside of me during this time. But as they prayed I was aware that I could choose life or death—that much was clear to me. I saw a dark tunnel with a light flickering at its far end. I told the Lord that I wasn't yet ready to die. Then, miraculously, I came to, with excruciating pain in the back of my head, where there was a lump the size of a grapefruit. After more prayer that afternoon, the lump completely disappeared. I was healed.

"Two weeks later, during personal prayer, the Lord gave me an interpretation of the tunnel vision: 'Do not walk in darkness, walk in light.' My life was radically changed through the experience and vision. Also, I know of at least two people who have decided to become Christians after I told them what happened to me that day in the Sierra Nevada."

It cannot be proved scientifically that Bill Pahl was raised from the dead. But there is an indisputable fact in his story: members of his small group did not hesitate to pray that God raise Bill from the dead. They were confident that God could work that way today, because Jesus had demonstrated his reign over death nineteen hundred years earlier.

7. Signs and Wonders in the Early Church

When first-century Christians came to a new town, signs and wonders followed. Starting at Pentecost, power evangelism swept the Mediterranean, demonstrating that the kingdom of God had come. From Jerusalem to Rome, from Asia to Europe; among Jews, Samaritans, and Gentiles; in every town, culture, and race, God's rule was established. We should not be surprised at this: a major part of Christ's ministry was devoted to training the disciples to do the Father's works, to preparing them to lead the church that was created at Pentecost.

But Christ's method of training is difficult for Western Christians to understand. There are several reasons for this. Evangelicals emphasize accumulating knowledge about God through Bible study. Christ was more action oriented; his disciples learned by doing as he did.

I have always found it rather odd that scientific Bible study, the historical-critical method, was not a key element in Christ's method of discipleship—odd, because scientific Bible study is the foremost, if not exclusive, method of training among Western evangelicals today, especially in our seminaries. The historical-critical method employs history, linguistics, and historical theology to discover what Scripture meant to its first-century audience. The method rightly assumes that what God intended to say to first-century Christians is what he intends for us also.

But there are problems related to the historical-critical method and the discipleship process. The first is that reliance on an intellectual method within a classroom-oriented structure skews the goal of the discipleship process toward intellectual formation and away from moral and spiritual formation. As we shall see, Christ's method of training was rabbinic, more oriented toward learning a way of life through doing than through the accumulation of knowledge about God.

The second problem is that evangelicals tend to rely on this method alone for character formation. This leads to an intellectual understanding of Christianity. If the historical-critical method were used as one tool among many, there might not be the current tendency toward the intellectualization of the Christian faith. But this is not usually the case.

"The historical-critical method," says New Testament scholar Russell P. Spittler, "when applied to Scripture, is both legitimate and necessary—but inadequate, . . . inadequate because . . . the end of biblical study cannot consist in historical dates or tentative judgments about complicated and conjectured literary origins. The end of biblical study consists rather in enhanced faith, hope, and love both for the individual and the community. The historical-critical method is inadequate, in other words, because it does not address piety." For Spittler, an important element of piety is God speaking through Scripture and prayer.[1]

The last problem involves the effect the historical-critical method has on the process of Bible study. Scripture study needs to proceed in the spirit of faith, hope, and love. By its nature, the historical-critical method is a rigorous intellectual task. The student easily falls into reliance on study rather than reliance on the Holy Spirit. Christ based his training on Scripture, and the goal of his training was piety, learning to hear God's voice and do his bidding.

Among Western Christians, another obstacle to understanding Christ's method of discipleship is the rejection of signs and wonders today. Signs and wonders, all Western evangelicals acknowledge, were necessary to authenticate Christ's divinity. Further, signs and wonders were key in establishing the apostolic authority of the Twelve and Paul. But most Western Christians reject or adopt a generally negative attitude

toward signs and wonders after the first century. This dimin-
ishes the effectiveness of Christ's example for us and discounts
much of what Christ intended that we do. What Christians—
including evangelicals—are often left to follow is a good moral
example, not a dynamic, Satan-conquering Lord. This results
in overly intellectual disciples—certainly not a people who
cause demons to tremble.

A closer look at how Jesus trained the disciples to do signs
and wonders and how they carried on that ministry after
Christ's ascension reveals many of the key elements for practicing power evangelism today.

A MOTLEY CREW

Signs and wonders were the proof of Jesus' messiahship,
the calling cards of the kingdom of God. Their presence in the
early church demonstrates that Jesus intended them to be an
integral part of the disciples' ministry.

The disciples learned from Jesus how to do the works of the
kingdom. They might not have always understood the purpose
of his miracles, but they learned how to do signs and wonders
with remarkable success. Jesus' method of instruction was the
method of the day: rabbinic. A rabbi would minister while his
disciples watched; then they would minister with him watching; next they went out on short missions, reporting back for
further instruction and correction from the master. After re-
peating this process for years and the rabbi was convinced his
disciples were formed in *his* way of life, he released his students to become rabbis and teach others by the same process.

Christ used this same training method with his disciples.
Christ, the Teacher, Rabbi, formed his disciples in *his* way of
life, passing on his character. Faith, hope, love, joy, peace, and
so on were the goals of his training. Performing signs and
wonders—casting out demons, healing the sick, even walking
on water—were avenues through which the disciples learned
more about God's nature. The disciples understood and accepted what Jesus expected of them. We never read of them

objecting to being *asked* to do the works of Jesus, only of their sense of personal inadequacy in performing his commands.

In the early years of my upbringing I often visited a horse farm in Illinois where my grandfather worked. He trained Tennessee walking horses. Tennessee walkers have a remarkable high-strutting gait, different from any other horse in the world. One day I was with him while he worked on a horse with a problem gait. His solution was to hitch a pacer—a horse with the correct gait—to the horse with the problem and let them walk together. After a few days, the problem horse's gait became consistent, just like the pacer's. My grandfather explained that when a horse cannot do its job, if you connect it to one that can, soon both do the job correctly.

I have been training men and women for twenty-five years. During this period I have learned that the secret for success with people is the same as with horses: hitch a person who cannot do a job with one who can, and soon both will know how. This is how Christ trained the Twelve: they lived with him, soon living like him. Power evangelism works the same way. Being around someone who does it successfully is the best way to learn to do it yourself.

The primary criterion for becoming one of the Twelve was a willingness to follow Christ—to walk with him, and to choose to become like him. Other than that desire, the only thing the disciples had in common was that they were Jews with middle-class economic and social standing living in Galilee. (Judas was the exception; the others were mostly fishermen.) From a human perspective, one can imagine the Father telling his Son, "If we can train this motley crew to advance my kingdom, we can train anyone." This gives all of us hope.

Through mutual commitment, Jesus made disciples out of the Twelve. He developed mature character and leadership in them. He trained them to do signs and wonders. They were hitched together for three years, and when released, the disciples continued to walk in his way. They performed signs and wonders and trained the next generation to perform them also.

But the disciples had difficulty in learning to do signs and wonders. They often misunderstood Christ's teachings (Matt. 13:36; 15:15; 16:6–12). They never fully understood his mission until after the resurrection—and even then they were in need of further correction (Mark 8:31–32; 9:31–32; Acts 1:8). They also misunderstood his authority as it related to the kingdom of God (Mark 10:35–40; Luke 9:46–48). But Jesus was patient with them, for his goal was to build men who did the Father's bidding.

For three years, the Twelve were in a learning environment. They not only learned new ideas but they developed new skills and abilities. They were teachable because they saw a large gap between Christ's life and their own. Progressive growth came through trial and error.

Frequent failures characterized the early ministry of all the disciples (Luke 9:37–43, 52–55), especially Peter's. His abortive attempt to walk on water (Matt. 14) is one of many examples. As the disciples continued to live with Christ, their failures diminished and their successes became more frequent. Each new step of faith was a springboard for their Master to push them further, enlarging their worldview and expanding their understanding of God.

FAITH IN THE MIRACULOUS

Perhaps the most difficult lesson the disciples learned was how to have faith that produces miracles. Maybe I am overly sensitive to this because I had such difficulty learning about this type of faith. I think not, though.

For example, consider the feeding of the five thousand (Mark 6:33–44). This is one of the greatest miracles in the New Testament. Several points about faith can be learned from this episode that help with the practice of power evangelism.

First, Jesus was motivated by compassion. "When Jesus landed and saw a large crowd, he had compassion on them, because they were like sheep without a shepherd." Jesus' divine compassion, supernatural mercy, frequently precipitated his works. (Moved by compassion, he healed, taught, performed miracles, raised the dead, and expelled demons. See Matt. 20:34; Mark 1:41; 5:19; 6:34; 8:2–10; Luke 7:11–17). We too need to ask God for his compassion.

Second, Jesus, listening to his Father, did not yield to the apostles' wish to send the crowd away. The apostles, observing the people's hunger and their lack of immediate resources, concluded that the crowd should be dispersed. Their solution was quite reasonable; they gave no thought to a miraculous provision. But if Jesus had acceded to their suggestion to disperse the crowd, one of the greatest miracles recorded in Scripture would have been lost. I wonder how many times we "rationally and reasonably" miss miracles today? Jesus listened to the Father—not the disciples—and the miracle was performed.

Third, Jesus used the disciples' spiritual blindness on this occasion to train them in signs and wonders. "You give them something to eat" is his response to their suggestion to disperse the crowd. This of course gave the apostles cause to reexamine their resources: five loaves and two fish. It was a crucial moment in their training. They were being told to do something for which they did not have adequate resources. I have discovered that praying for the healing of a blind person accomplishes the same thing to me. I know my own resources are inadequate. Miracles occur through our inadequacy, the crucible in which faith is formed.

Fourth, Jesus gave instructions to the disciples and they obeyed. He told them to organize the crowd "in groups of hundreds and fifties." They had no idea where the food was to come from; nevertheless they prepared the people to receive. We are in the same position today: we need to listen to and act on Jesus' instructions, even when we cannot see the provision.

Finally, the miracle of multiplication of the bread and fish probably occurred in the apostles' hands as well as Christ's.

He had commanded the apostles to "give them something to eat" (Mark 6:37). Many commentators believe that the miracle of multiplication occurred only in the hands of Jesus. They may be correct, but the passage leaves room for thinking the miracle happened in the disciples' hands as well as Christ's— just as with exorcism and healing.

It is a possible interpretation that the apostles were handed, after Christ's blessing, a meager portion of bread and fish. Then they went into the crowd and began passing it out and the multiplication occurred before their eyes. The miracle was in their hands and hearts. They learned that multiplication could occur through them. Only God can work miracles, but he often does it by the hands of Christians.

We must do better than the apostles in learning from this miracle. Later, after Jesus walked on the water, Mark says, "They were completely amazed, for they had not understood about the loaves; their hearts were hardened" (Mark 6:51–52). Jesus had to show the Twelve again and again how to perform signs and wonders. With the help of the Holy Spirit and with soft hearts, we can avoid some of their failures.

TRANSFERRING MINISTRY

In Luke 9:1–2 we read, "When Jesus had called the Twelve together, he gave them power and authority to drive out all demons and to cure diseases, and he sent them out to preach the Kingdom of God and to heal the sick." He was sending the disciples as his personal ambassadors; thus they went in his authority and power.

Their commissioning is analogous to being a train engineer. Train engineers direct powerful machines, and success depends on working within specific schedules, on the right tracks, and at the proper speeds. Too often we think the authority and power of God is a carte blanche to do whatever we want, more like driving an automobile than a train. In fact, the commission to the Twelve came with stringent limitations: they were only to do the will of the Father.

When he sent them, Jesus provided the disciples with practical instructions. He told them where and to whom they should go. They were to proclaim the kingdom of God to recipients, freely offering healing—no matter what the needs—because they themselves had received freely. A simple life-style of trusting God and owning few material possessions (for freedom of movement) was observed. They received hospitality and material support of people receptive to their message and avoided wasting time with those who rejected the kingdom. Persecution was expected, so they were taught to operate wisely yet keep their innocence (not an easy task, though Christ's life was their pattern). In all instances Jesus' Spirit would help and instruct them.

Even though given the authority and power of the kingdom of God, the Twelve still had to exercise it. Power, I too have learned, comes as we exercise what God has given. The disciples could give only what they had received, but in giving they received more. Until they actually healed the sick and cast out demons, their authority and power meant little to them.

The Twelve encountered difficulties, though at first their excursions were successful—even the demons were subject to them! Soon, however, they faced difficulties with their own pride and carnality. For example, they tried to stop others who were healing in Jesus' name, and they lapsed into unbelief. They also experienced persecution from religious leaders.

In Luke 9:41, we read of Christ's response to the disciples' failure, in this case their inability to cast a demon from a child: "O, unbelieving and perverse generation, how long shall I stay with you and put up with you?" Jesus was frustrated with their lack of faith. It was very important to him that they learn how to cast out all demons, so when he departed from earth that ministry would continue.

Christ delivered the boy of the evil spirit immediately, using the occasion to teach the disciples that soon they would not have his help. "Listen carefully to what I am about to tell you: The Son of Man is going to be betrayed into the hands of men" (Luke 9:44). They needed to learn about faith for deliverance, because he was soon to leave them.

Signs and wonders were done through the followers' faith, quickened by the guidance of the Holy Spirit. When with Jesus, the disciples were trained in faith for miracles. When Peter and John healed the lame man at the gate called Beautiful, Peter explained that it was not because of their spirituality; faith in Jesus' name made the man whole (Acts 3:1–10). This assertive faith has confidence without need of proof or regard for evidence, a willingness to stand by what God commands. (I do not imply that we claim someone is healed when symptoms of illness are still present. Faith for healing means that we believe God is able to heal specific persons today, and there is a specific sense of God's working.)

The expansion of the ministry of signs and wonders from the One to many has cosmic effects. When Jesus sent out the Twelve, and later the Seventy-two, he increased the possibilities for people's deliverance from the devil. The kingdom of darkness suffered defeat. The expansion of the kingdom of God—and accompanying defeat of Satan—is affected by the number of Christians performing signs and wonders.

ACCOMPANYING SIGNS

For three years Jesus taught the disciples how to minister from hearts of compassion and mercy, hear the Father, grow in dependence on the Holy Spirit, be obedient to God's leading, and believe that God performs miracles through men and women. Even though they frequently forgot or misunderstood what they were taught, his post resurrection commission, as recorded in Mark 16:14–20, was consistent with their training:

Jesus appeared to the Eleven as they were eating; he rebuked them for their lack of faith . . . [and he] said to them, "Go into all the world and preach the good news to all creation. . . . And these signs will accompany those who believe: In my name they will drive out demons; they will speak in new tongues; they will pick up snakes with their hands; and when they drink deadly poison, it will not hurt them at all; they will place their hands on sick people, and they will get well."

. . . Then the disciples went out and preached everywhere, and the Lord worked with them and confirmed his word by the signs that accompanied it.

I find it remarkable that many Western Christians are surprised at the emphasis on signs and wonders in this commissioning. Yet the way the disciples fulfilled the great commission indicates Christ's commitment to power evangelism, a key part of their training.

Some have challenged the genuineness of Mark 16:9–20. While it is true that several of the most reliable early manuscripts do not contain this passage, all Christian traditions have included it in the canon of Scripture. But even if the passage is excluded from the canon, we cannot disregard the overwhelming evidence that the early disciples in fact fulfilled the Mark commission: they cast out demons, spoke in tongues, picked up snakes, and healed the sick. If the passage was not in the original text, another question arises. Why was such a text added—if it were, as evidence suggests (not confirms)—in the second century?

Luke was the theologian of the Holy Spirit. In the first chapter of Acts, he wrote that Acts was a companion volume to his Gospel. The purpose of his Gospel was to write all that Jesus did and taught (Acts 1:1). In Acts, Luke continued the story of Jesus' works and teaching, only now it was done by the disciples (Acts 1:8).

Luke began the book of Acts by contrasting the disciples before Pentecost with the empowered group after. In chapter 1, the disciples still operated according to Old Testament principles. They misunderstood Christ's mission (Acts 1:6); they chose Judas's replacement by casting lots, recalling the Urim and Thummin of the Old Testament. After the Spirit came and someone needed to be chosen to fill an office again, they used different methods (see Acts 6:1–6). The training they received in discipleship came together with the catalytic outpouring of God's Spirit at Pentecost. Power evangelism was unleashed on the world.

There are at least ten kinds of sign phenomena in the book of Acts that produced evangelistic growth in the church. They are specifically called "signs and wonders" nine times and include healing, expelling demons, miracles with nature and food, resuscitation of the dead, and being transported from one place to another. "The apostles performed many miraculous signs and wonders among the people. . . . [And] more and more men and women believed in the Lord and were added to their numbers" (Acts 5:12, 14).[2] One power encounter is mentioned between Paul and Elymas in Salamis on the island of Cyprus. The result was the proconsul believed (13:4–12). The following is an incomplete summary, though I added footnotes with more detailed references for further investigation:

Speaking gifts. Tongues and prophecy occur four times in Acts, three as a result of which the church grew. For example, at Pentecost the disciples were "filled with the Holy Spirit and began to speak in other tongues as the Spirit enabled them," resulting in "about three thousand [being] added to their number that day" (2:4, 41).[3]

Visions. There are four instances of visions. Cornelius, the Caesarean centurian, received a vision—an answer to his prayers—and was told to send for Peter. The next day, Peter had a related vision. The two visions resulted in the gospel being preached to the Gentiles for the first time, with many responding by being baptized (see 10:1, 9, 47).[4]

Dead raised. Two resuscitations are recorded. The first is Dorcas (or Tabitha, as she was called in Aramaic); Peter raised her from the dead, resulting in "many people [believing] in the Lord" (9:40–42). The second is Eutychus, raised from the dead by Paul, with no recorded evangelistic result (20:7–12).

Assorted miracles. There are six specific miracles recorded. On the island of Malta a viper bit Paul and he suffered no ill effects. According to church tradition, the people responded to the miracle by believing in Christ, and the church was established (28:3–10).[5]

There were also phenomena that were likened to miracles of nature. For example, the opening of the gates for Peter in the twelfth chapter; the earthquake, unfastened fetters, and opened doors in the sixteenth chapter; and the sound like wind and tongues like fire in the second chapter. The last phenomena helped account for three thousand converts.

Healings. There are seven specific healings. Paul healed Aeneas's paralysis, resulting in the conversion of the towns of Lydda and Sharon (Acts 9:32–43).[6]

Angelic visitations. There are three recorded visitations. An angel told Philip to go to a desert road south of Jerusalem; there he evangelized the Ethiopian eunuch (Acts 8:26–40). According to church tradition, the eunuch returned to Ethiopia and established the church.[7]

Signs and wonders occurred fourteen times in the book of Acts in conjunction with preaching, resulting in church growth.[8] Further, on twenty occasions church growth was a direct result of signs and wonders performed by the disciples. Rarely was church growth attributed to preaching alone.

What conclusions can be drawn from my brief survey of the books of Acts? First, the early church—particularly the Twelve—carried on Christ's ministry, and this included signs and wonders. They were trained by Christ in how to do them, and they did them well.

Second, not only the Twelve healed the sick, cast out demons, and experienced visions. Other Christians did too. Signs and wonders were a part of daily life, expected by the church. Paul, Stephen, Cornelius, Ananias—none of them members of the original Twelve—all practiced signs and wonders.

Finally, signs and wonders resulted in dramatic church growth. They were the catalyst for evangelism.

SIGNS AND WONDERS AND CHURCH HISTORY

Signs and wonders did not cease with the close of the New Testament canon. They have continued to occur throughout history. Reliable documents from every century of church history demonstrate that prophecy, healing, deliverance, and tongues have not disappeared from the Christian experience (see Appendices A and B).

Among theologians and historians today we find a variety of perspectives about the validity of signs and miracles. These positions influence how writers treat reports of miracles. J. Sidlow Baxter in his book *Divine Healing of the Body* describes four positions held by modern Christians about signs and wonders in postbiblical history.[9]

Signs and wonders ceased at the end of the apostolic age, around the end of the first century. Reformed theologian B. B. Warfield in his book *Counterfeit Miracles* thought the supernatural gifts "were confined to the apostolic age, and to a very narrow circle then." Their purpose was to establish the authority of the apostles; once accomplished, the charismatic gifts were done away with.

According to Warfield's position, signs and wonders reported after that time were, a priori, either spurious or did not occur by divine means. This is a circular argument, in which a theological judgment is made that signs and wonders are impossible after the first century, forcing the conclusion that historical evidence is fraudulent. The great weakness of Warfield's position is he cannot use Scripture to support his contention that divine miracles ceased upon the death of the apostles and their generation. No Scripture passage either states or implies his position. (For a discussion of 1 Cor. 13:10, see Chapter 8.)

Signs and wonders ceased because they belonged only to the earliest centuries of the church. According to this theory, they were no longer needed to validate the gospel. The church, once widely established and officially sanctioned, was enough to certify the authenticity of the Christian message. The cutoff date is the time of the completion of the canon, usually recognized to have been at the Council of Carthage in 397.

This argument accepts second- and third-century documentation of signs and wonders, arbitrarily assigning their early cessation. But why a particular cutoff? When was the church widely established and officially sanctioned? Is 397 when the canon was closed? (Many historians would dispute that conclusion.) Where does Scripture teach this?

Signs and wonders faded and ceased as leaders of the organized church opposed them. This argument, which contradicts the church establishment theories above, has some merit. In fact, as faith for miracles wanes, especially among pastoral leaders, miracles decrease in frequency. Also, when unusual signs and wonders have occurred—events that often threaten the hierarchy and status quo of the church—leadership has tended to inhibit them.

There have been waves of signs and wonders throughout church history, and the hierarchy has alternately retarded or encouraged their ebb and flow. But the main point of this argument—that the gifts have completely ceased—cannot stand up to the historical test. It cannot be documented that the gifts have ceased for any significant period of time in church history, especially today.

Signs and wonders have never ceased. They have occurred from the apostolic age until now, in varying degrees. This last position is supported by Scripture and church history.

After the Enlightenment and with the advent of nineteenth-century theological liberalism church leaders resisted signs and wonders. They denied the *possibility* of supernatural intervention in creation. Theological secularists, as I prefer to call them, do not fit into any of Baxter's categories. They deny the possibility of even first-century signs and wonders. They are, sadly, materialists cloaking their philosophy with religious language.

How have positions that deny signs and wonders become popular among Western Christians, including orthodox, historic Christians? Why the skepticism toward or overt ridicule of reports of miracles? The next chapter tells why.

8. The Next Stage

C. Peter Wagner, in a 1983 interview, predicted a new stage (or "third wave," as he calls it) of the Holy Spirit's work in this century. The first, Dr. Wagner noted, was the Pentecostal movement at the turn of the century. The second, popularly known as the charismatic renewal, began in the sixties and touched mainline Protestants and Catholics. He predicted a third wave affecting evangelical Protestants.[1]

I believe Dr. Wagner's "third wave" is not so much another wave as the next stage of development in the charismatic renewal. Perhaps both the Pentecostal and charismatic movements are part of one great movement of the Holy Spirit in this century. In this perspective the similarities between the movements outweigh their differences.

There is much to learn from the first two movements in this century. "If it weren't for the charismatic movement and also the classical Pentecostals," Dr. Wagner noted, "we who are neither one of those would probably never have even heard of the power of the Holy Spirit. So what we are doing is certainly attributable to the way in which God is working in them. What I see is a lowering of traditional barriers between those of us who are evangelicals, and charismatics and Pentecostals, so that we can have the same results, the same work of the Holy Spirit in both groups, even though we tend to explain what is happening in a slightly different way."[2]

In preparation for my course at Fuller Seminary on the miraculous and church growth, I studied both the Pentecostal and charismatic movements. I discovered why, despite holding a similar theology, the two are different: each of these movements has affected different groups of people. These groups are culled from different economic, social, religious, and educational pools. As would be expected, the nature of each movement is also quite different.

PENTECOSTALISM

The modern Pentecostal movement started at the April 1906 Azusa Street revival in Los Angeles, California. Thomas Ball Barratt (the "apostle of Pentecost" to Western Europe) brought the Azusa Street revival back to his church in Oslo, Norway, in December 1906. From there it spread quickly to the United Kingdom. For church growth in this century Pentecostals far outstrip all other Christian groups. Of the 345 million Protestants worldwide, by 1980 Pentecostals comprised the largest denominational subgroup, with over 51 million members. (There are 49.8 million Anglicans, 47.5 million Baptists, and 43.4 million Lutherans.)[3]

Growth in individual Pentecostal denominations and churches highlights this trend. For example, the Assemblies of God began in 1914 with about ten thousand members and today claims over ten million members worldwide.[4] Since 1964, the Church of God in Christ, the largest predominantly black Pentecostal denomination in America, has grown from 450,000 to 3,700,000 members.[5] According to church growth specialist Elmer Towns, four of the ten largest congregations in the world are now Pentecostal, including the three largest: the Full Gospel Central Church (500,000) in Seoul, Korea; the Jotabeche Church (100,000) in Santiago, Chile; and the Congregacao Crista (61,250) in Sao Paulo, Brazil.[6]

Not only do these statistics indicate spectacular growth, missiologists believe the numbers could grow much larger. For example, in Latin America C. Peter Wagner projects Pentecostal numbers could increase *fivefold* over the next fifteen years. (In 1969, sixty-three percent of all Latin American Protestants were Pentecostals.[7]) Here is the overall Protestant trend in Latin America:

In 1900 there were about fifty thousand Protestants in all of Latin America.

In the 1930s growth passed the one million mark.

In the 1940s growth passed the two million mark.

In the 1950s growth passed the five million mark.

In the 1960s growth passed the ten million mark.

In the 1970s growth passed the twenty million mark.

Some statisticians project around a hundred million Protestants in Latin America for the year 2000.[8]

Dr. Wagner believes the Pentecostal proportion has increased since 1969, meaning there could be between sixty-five and seventy-five million Pentecostals in Latin America alone by the year 2000! One conclusion that can be drawn from these statistics is that churches grow when the power of God is released. "Ignorance of spiritual gifts," Dr. Wagner notes, "may be a chief cause of retarded church growth [in North America] today. It also may be the root of much of the discouragement, insecurity, frustration, and guilt that plagues many Christian individuals and curtails their effectiveness for God."[9] Pentecostals' large (and growing) numbers seem to substantiate Wagner's statement.

Over the years Pentecostalism has come under attack from both secular and Christian groups. A closer look at Pentecostal roots reveal one reason why: social differentiation. The 1906 Azusa Street revival was led by an uneducated black holiness preacher, William J. Seymour, who attracted a poor, mostly black congregation. (The holiness movement, dating from the mid-nineteenth century, tried to preserve the original thrust of the Methodist teachings on entire sanctification and Christian perfection as taught by John Wesley.) In my investigations of the Pentecostal healing revivalists and evangelists of the past forty years, I discovered many of the men and women came from poverty stricken surroundings and may have been affected by the associated traumas of broken homes and substance abuse. Few had much formal education. I have always wondered if racism and social snobbishness lay behind the early attacks on Pentecostals.

Pentecostal historian Vinson Synan in his book *In the Latter Days* outlines five fronts on which Pentecostals encountered opposition:

Criticism by the press. These attacks, from both the secular and Christian press, continue today. They usually depict Pentecostal meetings as wildly emotional, with people losing control, screaming, rolling around in the aisles, babbling like idiots— a spectacle for the rest of the world to watch. Reports of physical healings are usually questioned in such a way as to lead readers to infer they were staged.[10]

Violent attacks. During the first half of the century bigots and hoodlums without specifically religious concerns, who were often worked up by reports from the press threatened or mugged Pentecostal preachers. They would disrupt meetings, burn down tents and churches, and even attempt to kill Pentecostals, as was the case for Oral Roberts in 1947 in Tulsa, Oklahoma.[11]

Criticism and rejection from holiness and fundamentalist Christians. These Christians, with whom the Pentecostals agreed on almost every major doctrine of faith, were their most bitter enemies. The most severe of these critics claimed Pentecostals were of Satan. G. Campbell Morgan called the movement "the last vomit of Satan."[12] (I will discuss in greater detail their theological concerns later in this chapter and also in Chapter 9.) In 1919, to disassociate itself from Pentecostalism, the Pentecostal Church of the Nazarene repudiated and dropped the word "Pentecostal" from its name to become the Church of the Nazarene, as it is still known today. Other denominations that denounced Pentecostals included the Wesleyan Church, the Church of God (Anderson, Indiana), the Salvation Army, and the Free Methodist Church. Because they were rejected by their denominations (in many cases even excommunicated), Pentecostals formed new churches.

Psychological and sociological rationalizations. While those from holiness and fundamentalist circles attacked from a theological perspective, many early twentieth-century liberals, especially university and seminary professors, used modern psychology and sociology to slander Pentecostals. Pentecostal phenomena, they said, could be explained by "mental instability, madness, poverty, repression of the sex drive, ignorance, and lower-class behavior."[13] These early studies have been discounted, in most cases because the authors' understanding of psychology or sociology has been outdated as new theories have corrected or replaced old theories. In fact, Synan points out, later studies of Pentecostals that compare them with control groups made up of those not speaking in tongues indicate the Pentecostals are as or more stable emotionally than the control group.[14]

Serious theological and exegetical criticism. Since the sixties, serious scholars, unlike earlier critics, have accepted many points of Pentecostalism with the exception of the doctrine of "total sanctification" (which not all Pentecostals believe) and the initial evidence theory of tongues.[15] What is significant about this group of critics, Synan notes, is that they take Pentecostals seriously, accepting them as brothers and sisters.

In addition to Synan's observations, some Pentecostal revivalists (especially those not associated with any church) have been criticized because of instability in their ministries and personal lives. Their problems—all too often reported by the press, secular and Christian—include mishandled finances, exaggerated claims regarding attendance at meetings and numbers and kinds of healings, and an exalted view of their ministries.

Not until 1943 in the United States, when the National Association of Evangelicals offered membership to several Pentecostal denominations, were Pentecostals accepted by conservative evangelicals. Even then, it was not until the seventies, with the advent of the charismatic renewal and as an effect of the Assemblies of God's Thomas F. Zimmerman's ecclesiastical statesmanship, which made Pentecostals into regularized evangelicals, that serious dialogue and cooperation between the two groups occurred.

THE CHARISMATIC RENEWAL

According to David Barrett in his massive *World Christian Encyclopedia* over 11 million people today are *practicing* members of the charismatic renewal.[16] Further, a 1979 Gallup Poll commissioned by *Christianity Today* magazine indicated that eighteen percent of all Roman Catholics over eighteen years of age in the United States *consider themselves* charismatics. In the same poll, among Lutherans, Methodists, Baptists, and Presbyterians, from sixteen to twenty percent considered themselves charismatics. In December of 1985 EP News Service reported that 22 of the nation's 336 Catholic bishops, and over 1500 parish priests, consider themselves charismatic. About five percent of the nation's Episcopal clergy describe themselves as charismatic.

The charismatic renewal differs in many respects from the Pentecostal movement. The reasons for this lie in its origins and leadership, both quite removed from Pentecostalism. I studied about leaders like Dennis Bennett, Father Ralph Diorio, Father John Bertolucchi, Larry Christenson, Kevin and Dorothy Ranaghan, Ralph C. Martin, Dennis and Matthew Linn, Francis MacNutt, Father Michael Scanlan, Sister Briege McKenna, Father Edward McDonough, Agnes Sanford, Michael Harper, Michael Green, and David Watson. At the time of this writing all except Agnes Sanford and David Watson are alive, reflecting the youth of the movement. Generally speaking, the leaders of the charismatic renewal are formally educated and are from stable families. They were raised in denominational churches and stayed within them, rather than moving out into independent style ministries.[17]

Charismatic leaders (evangelists, healers, teachers) minister from local church bases. Many are best described as "pastoral healers" because of their concern for pastoral follow-up to their ministry. They are usually pastors of or are closely tied in with congregations, though they may also travel extensively, conducting healing seminars and services. Their focus, even in their travels, is basically to members of their denomination. Because they maintain committed relationships and denominational loyalty, they usually have long-term success.

Finally, these charismatic leaders do not enjoy the evangelistic response from nonchurched people that the Pentecostals do, because charismatic ministries are focused in denominational churches. In fact, many members of Protestant and Catholic congregations experience personal conversion to Christ through the charismatic renewal. In this sense the renewal is thoroughly evangelistic, reaching nominal members of mainline churches. It is a renewal and reforming movement within mainline Protestant and Catholic churches—very different from Pentecostalism.

THE NEXT STAGE?

In 1980 I had a long, animated discussion about the charismatic renewal with David Watson. He was receiving reports that the charismatic renewal was over; some were even saying we were in a "postcharismatic" era. As evidence, he mentioned the decline in conference attendance, both in the United Kingdom and the United States, frequent divisions among leaders, and (more subjectively) a general malaise marked by discouragement and discontent.

It was not an encouraging report. Yet as he spoke I thought of the large increases in the number of Pentecostals and charismatics and wondered: have we entered a postcharismatic era or is the charismatic movement entering a new stage of its development? I believe a closer look at the British and American church scenes indicates the charismatic wave has not hit a breakwater. Instead, it continues to grow, no longer the institutional pariah of its early days.

Some are tempted to pronounce the charismatic renewal dead because it lacks youthful vitality. True, the early stages of the renewal are over. What we have now is a movement entering late adolescence, if not early adulthood. In order to understand this new stage in its development, we must look at what the charismatic renewal accomplished during its nascent phase.

In most denominations, the charismatic renewal has affected four areas of church life. First, the charismatic renewal has introduced new forms of worship by using dance, theater, innovative hymnody, and (in some instances) singing in tongues. Alive, joyful music is one of the most significant contributions the charismatic movement has made to the church.

Second, the charismatic renewal has led the way in renewed social experiences, especially in small groups, innovative discipleship, and Christian community. (Other Christians, such as Keith Miller, Robert Girard, Ronald Sider, Ray Stedman, and Gene Getz, have contributed to these efforts too.)

Third, the charismatic renewal has stimulated a revival of interest in the ministry of the Holy Spirit. In most mainline denominations, charismatic theology no longer raises the animosity it used to. Being charismatic is no longer controversial. We now find charismatic theologians among the Reformed, Lutherans, Catholics, Baptists, Presbyterians, Episcopalians and so on. In the United States, almost every mainline denomination has recognized charismatic renewal organizations, such as the Episcopal Renewal Ministries, the International Lutheran Renewal Center, the Presbyterian and Reformed Renewal Ministries, and the National Service Committee of the Catholic Charismatic Renewal.

Finally, the charismatic movement helped renew interest in personal disciplines like prayer, Bible study, meditation, and fasting. Again, I do not imply that charismatics can take credit for all the renewed interest in these disciples, only that they have played a significant part.

So the charismatic movement has taken root, burrowing into congregational structures, liturgy, and theology. Inevitably this has changed the renewal's character, not always for the good. Some dangers come with acceptance, perhaps the greatest danger being that with respectability easily comes a loss of leavening influence.

The charismatic renewal is at a crossroads: will it continue to be leaven in the churches, leading the way in spirituality, or will it become moribund as many renewal movements before it? For many renewal movements of the past (especially the Catholic orders), formal recognition and acceptance by the institution have been the seeds of their weakening. This raises a difficult question, because the unity of the body of Christ demands that a renewal movement work in concert with church leaders whenever possible. How can a renewal movement maintain its cutting edge when made a part of the institution? Perhaps all we can do is be aware of this danger and attempt to keep the renewal movement true to itself. (Of course, the longer a movement remains outside of the churches, the greater the chance for heresy or schism.)

There is another danger now facing the charismatic renewal. Acceptance by pastoral leaders does not imply permission to practice the gifts within the larger body. Many charismatics, though staying in their church denominations, have formed parachurch groups (approved by church leadership) in which they practice the charismatic gifts. Their acceptance within their denominations is circumscribed by keeping the gifts a private matter, away from the larger group. After time, though, isolation from the main body creates frustration. This often results in the loss of mainline membership into Pentecostal churches and the death of the parachurch groups. In fact, the loss of members to charismatic churches is one factor for mainline Protestant membership declines. (Among Catholics, one study indicates that involvement in the charismatic renewal brings inactive Catholics back into the church at a faster rate than involvement in the renewal encourages people to leave.)[18]

I do not know what can be done to retard the modest trend of charismatics leaving mainline Protestant congregations, but denominational leaders need to consider the problem more seriously. (The charismatic members' departure is probably a subpoint under the larger problem of exodus due to theological liberalism.) Among charismatics themselves, a concerted effort to work along with their noncharismatic evangelical brothers and sisters could be one way to exert greater influence in their denominations as well as to receive encouragement and support. Of course noncharismatic evangelicals must be willing to cooperate in this effort, something they have not always been eager to do.

THE EVANGELICAL KEY

One obstacle to greater evangelical unity has been labels: who are evangelicals and what are their subgroups? Evangelicals are a diverse group. Quoting from Michael Cassidy, "The term 'evangelical' describes the broad spectrum of Christians who limit religious authority to the Bible and who stress the New Testament doctrines of conversion, new birth, and justification by grace through faith alone. Evangelicals hold to the full inspiration of the Bible as the Word of God."[19] Under this broad definition, evangelicals include Pentecostals, charismatics, fundamentalists, and conservative evangelicals. We are sprinkled throughout mainline churches and concentrated in Pentecostal denominations, smaller, conservative evangelical denominations, and independent Bible congregations.

By *conservative evangelicals* I mean a subgrouping within evangelicalism that is noncharismatic but not necessarily anticharismatic. Charismatics and conservative evangelicals hold every major point of the Christian faith in common. Conservative evangelicals aggressively refute the influences of theological liberalism. Mainline liberals, not understanding the nuances of conservative evangelicals, often throw them together with their less tolerant fundamentalist cousins.[20] But this is a mistake, because conservative evangelicals as a group are more open to new ideas and relationships than are fundamentalists.

I believe a key element in the next stage of the charismatic renewal, one that appears already to be taking place, could be the coming together of these conservative evangelicals with charismatics and Pentecostals. This unity could do much for both groups. For charismatics, conservatives offer a rich theological heritage and concern for personal evangelism and missions. For conservative evangelicals, charismatics offer spiritual renewal, a deeper experience of God's working directly in their lives.

Theology is *very* important in one way or another for conservative evangelicals. Therein lies an obstacle to understanding signs and wonders: part of conservative evangelicals' theological heritage denies that the gifts function today.

So a major question that must be addressed to further conservative evangelical and charismatic unity is theological: the cessation theory of the charismatic gifts. The most popular conservative evangelical cessation theory is based on an interpretation of 1 Corinthians 13:10: " . . . but when *perfection* comes, the imperfect disappears." Conservative evangelicals teach that "perfection" in the verse refers to the completed canon of Scripture (the New Testament), recognized at the Council of Carthage in 397; "the imperfect" refers to the charismatic gifts, and they have "disappeared" or ceased. (See Chapter 6.)

Referring to the supernatural gifts, one author writes, "These [miracles, healings, tongues, and interpretation of tongues] were certain enablements given to certain believers for the purpose of authenticating or confirming God's word when it was proclaimed in the early church before the scriptures were penned. These sign gifts were temporary. . . . Once the Word of God was inscripturated, the sign gifts were no longer needed and they ceased."[21]

The argument for equating "perfection" with the closing of the New Testament canon has two parts. First, the word "perfection" is a neuter noun, and must, they imply, refer to a thing, not a person. Since Scripture is a thing and is neuter in gender, it follows that the Bible is the "perfect" to which Paul is referring. Second, this interpretation, they assert, fits well with verses 8, 9, 11, and 12 of the same passage in 1 Corinthians 13: " . . . where there are tongues, they will be stilled. . . . When I was a child, I talked like a child. . . . Now I know in part; then I shall know fully, even as I am fully known." In this line of reasoning, tongues are childish, while Scripture is mature.

There are several weaknesses with this interpretation, not the least of which is that a major doctrine is being built on a fairly unclear passage. Where else in Scripture is there a hint of this teaching?

Beyond this, while "perfection" is a neuter noun, in Greek there is no warrant for limiting its reference to another neuter noun. A neuter noun or pronoun can be used to describe masculine or feminine things or persons. One example is the Greek word translated "child" (*teknon*). Though neuter in gender, this noun may describe a little girl or boy. The point is that in the Greek—much like English—gender is grammatical, not sexual. The word "Spirit" (*pneuma*) is also a neuter noun, and Scripture is clear that the Spirit is not a thing but the Third Person of the Trinity.

Perhaps a bigger problem is that their interpretation calls for the leaving of the immediate context of 1 Corinthians 13 to determine the identity of "perfection." Instead, they jump to 2 Timothy 3:15–16, where "Scripture" is neuter. This is an arbitrary jump.

British scholar F. F. Bruce offers a more plausible interpretation of what "perfection" refers to: the second coming of Christ. This interpretation appears to fit well within the overall context of 1 Corinthians, especially 1:7: "Therefore you do not lack any spiritual gift as you eagerly wait for our Lord Jesus Christ to be revealed." [22]

It would be a mistake to think theology is the only obstacle to conservative evangelical and charismatic unity. In fact, I have discovered attempts to unify around theology are unsatisfying. Fear, for example, is another barrier. In particular there is the fear that the authority of Scripture will be undermined by gifts like prophecy and tongues, that subjective experience will replace objective truth as the plumb line of Christianity.

There also is a cultural barrier. Although not consciously understood, conservative evangelicals in recent years have moved up in social, economic, and educational status, making it harder to relate to Pentecostals.[23] Pentecostals too have been moving up the social scale, though not as rapidly as conservative evangelicals. On the other hand, many conservative evangelicals have been favorably affected by the charismatic renewal (by people of a social standing closer to theirs), even when, due to theological reservations, they have not experienced the gifts.

Perhaps the next stage of the Holy Spirit, one affecting conservative evangelicals, will come with different models of how the charismatic gifts should function, such as in power evangelism. Just as Pentecostalism and the charismatic renewal have produced different results as they affected different groups of people, this next stage of the charismatic renewal will have a different flavor, with a particular emphasis on personal evangelism. C. Peter Wagner reflects this thinking when he was asked if he considered himself a charismatic or Pentecostal:

I see myself as neither a charismatic nor a Pentecostal. I belong to Lake Avenue Congregational Church. I'm a Congregationalist. My church is not a charismatic church, although some of our members are charismatic.

However, our church is more and more open to the same way that the Holy Spirit does work among charismatics. For example, our pastor gives an invitation after every service for people who need physical healing and inner healing to come forward and go to the prayer room and be anointed with oil and prayed for, and we have teams of people who know how to pray for the sick.

We like to think that we are doing it in a Congregational way; we're not doing it in a charismatic way. But we're getting the same results.[24]

Conservative evangelicals frequently ask me questions about "the baptism of the Holy Spirit," a hallmark of Pentecostalism and the charismatic renewal. Is the term biblical? Does everyone have to speak in tongues? And what about the teaching that we do not have the Holy Spirit until we speak in tongues? How is the Pentecostal experience of the Holy Spirit related to conservative evangelical teaching on being filled with the Spirit? Answers to these questions are the topics of the next chapter.

9. Empowered by the Holy Spirit

In the summer of 1967 a friend of mind, Scott (not his real name), attended a students' retreat at Arrowhead Springs, California, the headquarters of Campus Crusade for Christ International. A nineteen-year-old U.C.L.A. student, he had been a committed Christian for five years, but his spiritual life had recently stalled. He was looking for more from God, something to empower his life and give clearer purpose.

Arrowhead Springs is carved into the mountains overlooking the city of San Bernardino. During an earlier era, it was an old health spa frequented by Hollywood stars; Greta Garbo and Clark Gable were reported to have sought "the cure" in sulphur-laced, steamy caverns deep below the main hotel. Perhaps, Scott thought, he would find a spiritual cure during this weeklong conference.

On arriving he discovered that he was to sleep in the hotel basement on a makeshift cot. Over seven hundred students from the United States and Canada jammed the facilities; it was not to be a Hollywood holiday. But that suited him well. It created an atmosphere of excitement and expectancy; if all these students came from hundreds and even thousands of miles away, surely God would show up!

The theme of the conference was personal evangelism. Toward the end of the week the students were to be transported on buses to local beaches where, going two by two, they would put into action what they had been taught—they would evangelize complete strangers.

Scott was apprehensive about going out, especially since he

had been raised on the beaches of southern California and was fearful of embarrassing encounters with old surfing buddies. Also, the idea of confronting complete strangers with a planned presentation became more frightening as the week progressed. At least, he soon discovered, they were not going to his home beach.

The evening before they went out, Dr. William Bright, president of Campus Crusade, presented a teaching about the Holy Spirit. His points were very simple: we cannot successfully live the Christian life in our own strength; the Father has sent the Holy Spirit to empower us; we are commanded in Scripture to "be filled with the Holy Spirit."

For years Scott had been taught not to focus on the Holy Spirit lest he weaken his relationship with Christ or fall into the excesses of the Pentecostals. This could be dangerous, leading possibly to deceit by the devil, even speaking in tongues. Besides, he heard many times, our primary purpose should be fulfilling the great commission. An emphasis on the Holy Spirit might detract us from this important task.

But Dr. Bright's talk stirred Scott deeply, allaying many of his fears. Dr. Bright said that only through the power of the Holy Spirit could we fulfill the great commission. (It was one of the few positive teachings Scott had ever heard on the Third Person of the Trinity.) "Perhaps," Scott mused, "this is the key to the refreshing I seek."

That night Scott could hardly sleep, intermittently awakening and thinking about Dr. Bright's words. By one o'clock he was wide-eyed, staring at the tangle of pipes and electrical tubing overhead, sensing God calling him to open his heart fully to the Holy Spirit. So he slipped out of bed, dressed, and found a quiet place under a lonely palm tree on the hotel grounds near an illuminated swimming pool.

Unsure of what to expect, his hunger for God motivated him to pray. "Holy Spirit," he pleaded, "I have been living in my own strength too long. Now I yield every part of my life to you. Come and fill me."

What happened next was outside of anything Scott had been taught about how God works. First, he felt a rush of power come over his body, a warm, tingling feeling he never had before experienced. With that rush came a peace and urging to worship God. As he began worshiping he was soon speaking in tongues, though initially he was unsure of what it was. After praying and worshiping for an hour he opened his Bible and began reading . . . and reading . . . and reading—late into the night. Scripture came alive; the very Word of God leapt off the pages.

The next day, knowing staff members were not sympathetic to charismatic phenomena, he told no one of his experience. Was it real? he wondered. It had to be. He was a different person, though confused about the meaning of what happened. As the time to go to the beaches approached, he noticed the gospel burned in his heart, pressing every part of his being with an urgency to tell others about Jesus Christ.

Scott boarded the bus without any fear, though he was still not looking forward to talking with strangers. But now he sensed his experience the night before would help him on the beaches.

His partner, Jim, a student at the University of North Carolina, was apprehensive. Scott knew that the Holy Spirit was telling him to take the lead on the beach. He quietly prayed as the bus snaked its way across the freeways leading to Newport Beach.

Newport Beach is typical of many beaches in southern California—sand covered with thousands of young people flocked around blasting radios, sharing the latest gossip, telling jokes, and watching other boys and girls walk by. Out into this mass of oily, tanning flesh went the God squads.

Scott and Jim first approached two Hispanic teenage boys, asking if they would mind participating in a religious survey (the survey was part of the evangelism program, a way of beginning conversation with strangers). Soon they were talking about Jesus Christ. Two girls joined the conversation, then another three boys. Scott had quickly put the Four Spiritual Laws aside and was telling the teenagers about their sins and God's grace. As he spoke he received insights about the teen-agers—sexual sins, problems with parents, problems at school—that were right on target. Supernaturally knowing what their greatest needs were, he spoke about God's love and righteous-ness in a way that opened their hearts. Jim stood by, astonished.

Within thirty minutes several of the teenagers were weep-ing, falling to their knees, repenting of their sins, and turning to Christ. Before the day was over at least a dozen young people made Christian commitments. In several instances stu-dents who initially joined the conversation only to mock and ridicule Scott ended on their faces, weeping, trembling, and repenting.

Whatever term one applies to what happened to Scott when he was overwhelmed by the Holy Spirit under the palm tree—filled, baptized, empowered—the result was power evange-lism. Sometimes, though, terminology is misleading and con-fusing. This discourages Christians from experiencing God's power in the way Scott did that night at Arrowhead Springs.

COMING TO TERMS

Andrew Murray, a nineteenth-century evangelical pastor and writer, wrote in his book *The Believer's Full Blessing of Pentecost*, "The greatest need of the church, and the thing which, above all others, believers ought to seek for with one mind and with their whole heart, is to be filled with the Spirit of God. . . . Every day ought to be a Pentecostal season in the church of Christ."[1] For many Christians (as was true for Scott and me) some of the greatest obstacles to "a daily Pentecost" are questions surrounding the pentecostal doctrine of "the baptism in (or of) the Holy Spirit."

The concept of being baptized in the Holy Spirit is a contro-versial doctrine. The term is found in Scripture, but over the past one hundred and fifty years Christians have understood its meaning in a variety of ways, almost always causing great misunderstanding and division among themselves.

Satan has been particularly effective in stirring up controversy over the Holy Spirit. Commenting on this problem, A. W. Tozer writes:

Satan has opposed the doctrine of the Spirit-filled life about as bitterly as any doctrine there is. He has confused it, opposed it, surrounded it with false notions and fears. He has blocked every effort of the Church of Christ to receive from the Father her divine and blood-bought patrimony. The church has tragically neglected this great liberating truth—that there is now for the child of God a full and wonderful and completely satisfying anointing with the Holy Spirit. The Spirit-filled life is not a special, deluxe edition of Christianity. It is part and parcel of the total plan of God for His people.[2]

In the nineteenth century, Methodists frequently used "baptism in the Holy Spirit" to refer to a postconversion experience, a "second blessing." In the eighteenth century John Wesley defined the second blessing as "entire sanctification." By this Wesley thought Christians could be perfected—the sinful nature eradicated—through a special second anointing of the Holy Spirit.[3] This is the hallmark doctrine of Wesleyan and holiness teaching, though only holiness Pentecostals today refer to it as the baptism of the Holy Spirit.[4]

By the turn of the century, the terms "baptism in the Holy Spirit" and "pentecostal" were popular among evangelicals outside of holiness circles. The baptism of the Holy Spirit was particularly emphasized in the writings of A. J. Gordon (the founder of Gordon College), F. B. Meyer, A. B. Simpson (the founder of the Christian and Missionary Alliance denomination), Andrew Murray, R. A. Torrey (the first president of Moody Bible Institute, Chicago), and evangelist Dwight L. Moody. This is how Moody described his baptism in the Holy Spirit:

I began to cry as never before, for a greater blessing from God. The hunger increased; I really felt that I did not want to live any longer. [He had been a Christian, and not only a Christian but a minister, and in charge of a mission for some time; he was getting conversions, but still he wanted more.] I kept on crying all the time that God would fill me with his Spirit. Well, one day in the city of New York— oh! what a day, I cannot describe it, I seldom refer to it. It is almost too sacred an experience to name. Paul had an experience of which he never spoke for 14 years. I can only say, God revealed himself to me, and I had such an experience of his love that I had to ask him to stay his hand.

Commenting on Moody's experience, D. Martyn Lloyd-Jones writes: "It was so overwhelming, he felt as if he was going to be physically crushed. The love of God! That is what is meant by 'the love of God in your hearts.' That is the baptism of the Spirit. That is what turned D. L. Moody from a good, regular, ordinary minister, into the evangelist who was so signally used of God in this and in other countries."[5]

Through these authors, a significant shift occurred in the understanding of the purpose of the Spirit's baptism. Along with Wesley's "entire sanctification," a second understanding arose with a new emphasis on anointing the Holy Spirit for witness and service. (This created a conflict with those who held the Wesleyan holiness doctrine.)

The new emphasis was spread through Keswick "Higher Life" conferences in England and their American counterpart in Massachusetts, Northfield Conferences, conducted by evanglist D. L. Moody. R. A. Torrey summarizes their teaching:

The baptism with the Holy Spirit is an operation of the Holy Spirit distinct from and subsequent from his regenerating work . . . an impartation of power for service. [This baptism was] not merely for the apostles, not merely for those of the apostolic age, but for "all that are afar off; even as many as the Lord our God shall call" . . . it is for every believer in every age of the church's history.[6]

While the late-nineteenth-century holiness and Keswick movements taught on the need of a baptism of the Holy Spirit for sanctification or empowering for service, they did not recognize the experience of charismatic gifts in the baptism. But R. A. Torrey, writing in 1895, wondered about this:

In my early study of the baptism with the Holy Spirit I noticed that in many instances those who were so baptized "spoke in tongues," and the questions often came into my mind, if one is baptized with the Holy Spirit will he not speak with tongues? But I saw no one so speaking and I often wondered, is there any one today who actually is baptized with the Holy Spirit?[7]

At this time the gift of tongues was rarely experienced, which explains Torrey's perplexed comment. But, as Pentecostal historian Vinson Synan has noted, "shouting, 'dancing in the spirit,' falling out 'under the power,' or catching the 'holy laugh' " were frequent phenomena at holiness gatherings.[8]

DIVISION

Understood against the background of nineteenth-century holiness and Keswick history (as well as parallel trends among Roman Catholics[9]), the early twentieth-century Pentecostal movement is not surprising. Beginning in 1901 at Charles Parham's Bethel Bible School in Topeka, Kansas, and the 1906 Azusa Street revival in Los Angeles, California, under William J. Seymour's leadership, large numbers of people spoke in tongues when prayed over for "the baptism in the Holy Spirit." There were other phenomena as well, including the expulsion of evil spirits, words of knowledge, healings, and prophecy.

Pentecostalism was born and with it yet another understanding of the term "baptism in the Holy Spirit." Soon the Pentecostals were teaching that through experiencing "the baptism of the Holy Spirit" Christians receive the Third Person of the Trinity. Further, it was thought that the initial evidence of receiving the Holy Spirit is speaking in tongues.

Pentecostals were and are divided on interpreting whether this experience is equated with Wesley's "entire sanctification" or Moody's "empowering for service."[10] For example, members of the Pentecostal Holiness Church fall within the former category, the Assemblies of God in the latter.

The development of early-twentieth-century Pentecostalism forced conservative evangelicals, who at that time frequently used the term "baptism in the Holy Spirit," to consider the charismatic gifts. By and large, those from both the holiness and Keswick traditions rejected the charismatic gifts. The conservative evangelicals claimed that the gifts ceased in the early church, that Pentecostalism was serious error, perhaps even demonic. Conservative evangelicals were especially offended by the teaching that tongues are the evidence of the baptism of the Holy Spirit, and that those who have not spoken in tongues do not have the Holy Spirit.

To disassociate themselves from the Pentecostals, conservative evangelicals avoided the term "baptism in the Holy Spirit." Instead, they used the term "filling" to describe believers' initial (and ongoing) experience of the Holy Spirit. As the Pentecostals continued to attract more people, many conservative evangelicals reacted, becoming more entrenched in their criticisms of Pentecostal doctrine. In many instances, to protect their people from what they considered serious error or excess of the Pentecostals, conservative evangelical pastors discouraged them from seeking any experience with the Holy Spirit.

At the same time dispensationalism, popularized through the Scofield Bible and the many pastors coming out of newly formed seminaries and Bible colleges, was growing in influence. Dispensationalists teach that God has dealt differently with men and women during different eras of biblical history. Of all theologies, dispensationalism is probably the most antagonistic toward the charismatic gifts and Pentecostalism.

Only in the past fifteen years have conservative evangelicals and Pentecostals begun serious dialogue regarding their differences over the Holy Spirit. Perhaps the key question (though by no means the only question) for both groups concerns the theological basis for our experience of the Holy Spirit. Conservative evangelicals have always taught that we should first establish the theological basis for activity, then explore the experience. As Pentecostalism and the charismatic renewal have grown, evangelicals have renewed their interest in the Holy

Spirit, in many instances changing negative attitudes toward the charismatic gifts. At the same time, Pentecostal theologians, perhaps through the influence of the charismatic renewal, are attempting more in-depth biblical reflection on the meaning of the baptism of the Holy Spirit. Both groups realize that resolution of the conflict is found in Scripture.

ONE BAPTISM, MANY FILLINGS

The concept of being baptized in the Holy Spirit originated with John the Baptist: "I baptize you with water. But one more powerful than I will come, the thongs of whose sandals I am not worthy to untie. *He will baptize you with the Holy Spirit* and with fire" (Luke 3:16). Later, at Christ's baptism, John proclaimed, " . . . the one who sent me to baptize with water told me, 'The man on whom you see the Spirit come down and remain is *he who will baptize with the Holy Spirit.*' I have seen and I testify that this [Jesus] is the Son of God" (John 1:33–34).

From these verses we learn that John taught that Israel should expect a new kind of baptizing with the coming of the Messiah.[11] John contrasted his baptizing with the Messiah's, which would come at a future, undisclosed time, and John's baptizing was with water, the Messiah's with the Holy Spirit.

In a postresurrection appearance, Jesus reminded the disciples of what John taught when he said, "John baptized with water, but in a few days you will be baptized with the Holy Spirit" (Acts 1:5). A few days later, at Pentecost, they were baptized with the Holy Spirit.

In explaining to his fellow apostles how the gift of the Holy Spirit was poured out on the Gentiles (something the apostles found difficult to accept), Peter said: "I remembered what the Lord had said, 'John baptized with water, but you will be baptized with the Holy Spirit.' So if God gave them the same gift as he gave us, who believed in the Lord Jesus Christ, who was I to think that I could oppose God?" (Acts 11:16).

The phrase employing the noun form for baptism—"*the baptism* of the Holy Spirit"—is not found in the New Testament. The verb form—"*being baptized* in the Holy Spirit"—is almost always used, with the lone exception of the words of Paul found in Acts 19:3—"What baptism did you receive?" But while the phrase "the baptism of the Holy Spirit" is not employed, the phenomenon John predicted, Christ said to expect, and occurs throughout Acts needs to be called by some name.

The English word "baptize" is transliterated from the Greek *baptizo*, which means to dip or immerse. It conveys the sense of being overwhelmed. John the Baptist, Jesus, and Peter all taught we should seek to be overwhelmed by the Spirit.

More confusing is that in the book of Acts being baptized in the Holy Spirit is equated with being "filled" with the Holy Spirit. "All of them," Luke says in Acts 2:4, "were *filled* with the Holy Spirit and began to speak in other tongues as the Spirit enabled them." This is one reason why conservative evangelicals are more comfortable describing the ongoing Christian experience of the Holy Spirit as a filling rather than a baptism.

I have discovered that the argument concerning the baptism of the Spirit usually comes down to a question of labels. Good medicine may be incorrectly labeled, which is probably true in this case. The Pentecostals' experience of God is better than their explanation of it. Unfortunately, the reverse can be true. It is possible to affirm orthodox theology, yet have little Christian character, service, and experience. An accurate label may adorn any empty bottle.

Terms like "the Trinity" and "receiving Christ as Savior" also are not found in the New Testament, yet few object to their use. Whether called "baptism" or "filling," God's gifts and power are essential for witness and service. All Christians are commanded to seek the Holy Spirit (see Eph. 5:18), regardless of how that experience is labeled. Still, the question remains, what is the best term to describe what John predicted and what then occurred in Acts?

Charles Hummel in *Fire in the Fireplace* points out that Paul and Luke used the term "baptism in the Holy Spirit" differently. Paul used it to mean an initial action of the Holy Spirit that incorporates the individual into the body of Christ at conversion (see especially 1 Cor. 12:13). Luke used it to mean an imbuing with power for effective witness and service, an experience that can be repeated.[12]

Clark Pinnock, commenting on Paul's and Luke's different usage, notes:

Baptism is a flexible metaphor, not a technical term. Luke seems to regard it as synonymous with "fulness" (Acts 2:4; cf. 11:16). Therefore, so long as we recognize conversion as truly a baptism in the Spirit, there is no reason why we cannot use "baptism" to refer to subsequent fillings of the Spirit as well. This latter experience, or experiences, should not be tied in with the tight "second blessing" schema, but should be seen as an actualization of what we have already received in the initial charismatic experience, which is conversion.[13]

Following this line of reasoning, which most conservative evangelicals agree with, the born-again experience is the consummate charismatic experience—what Paul would refer to as being baptized in the Holy Spirit. Any ensuing interaction between the individual and the Holy Spirit would come under the heading of "fillings," as taught by Paul. Further, these fillings may happen again and again—they are both initiatory and repeatable.

So, following Paul, it is probably best to speak of "being filled with the Holy Spirit." But in Luke we find warrant in using "being baptized with the Holy Spirit." Both terms convey the fact that it is urgent for Christians to seek sincerely the power of the Holy Spirit.

TIMING

When does our baptism or filling occur? As Pinnock comments, the filling is both initiatory (John 3:3–6) and repeatable

(Gal. 5:25). The Spirit's coming on the disciples at Pentecost annointed them to establish the church. Repeated fillings empowered them for prophecy, healing, apostleship, and so on. In the book of Acts, Peter was filled with the Holy Spirit twice (2:4, 4:31).

As we have need, God provides his Counselor (John 14:16, 26; 16:7, 13–15). Throughout the book of Acts, "Luke takes his subjects where he finds them and leaves them in a fully Spirit-baptized state, which is the same as to say they became true believers."[14] There is no identifiable pattern or "correct" sequence for being filled with the Spirit. "Completeness," theologican Russell Spittler notes, "and not subsequence, strikes me as a better category by which to understand the arrival of the Spirit in Acts."[15] Our concern too should not be *when* we experience the Spirit's filling but *that* we experience it.

I believe that when a person is converted he or she receives the Holy Spirit, although he or she may not experience the Holy Spirit at that time. Conversion and the initial filling experience of the Holy Spirit can happen simultaneously. Certainly the potential for that is there. In fact, I now frequently see people receive Christ and get filled with the Holy Spirit at the same time. Why? I teach that because the Holy Spirit is now in them, they may by faith actualize its power and gifts.

Anyone born again has the potential of experiencing the power and gifts of the Holy Spirit. We should expect this experience—Scripture teaches it is a part of the normal Christian life. If the experience of the Holy Spirit is not preached or seen by Christians—which is true in many evangelical churches—they will not expect these things to happen, and they will not happen. "Faith comes from hearing the message, and the message is heard through the word of Christ" (Rom. 10:17). As Christians learn and see that there is more to experience, they are willing to take a chance, step out in faith, and receive God's power.

When I talk with evangelicals about the Holy Spirit, I ask if when they were born again they received the Spirit. If they answer yes (and they should), I tell them all that remains is to *actualize* what the Spirit has, all that is required is to release the gifts. I then lay hands on them and say, "Be filled with the Spirit"—and they are.

I have discovered that when Pentecostals say Christians need "to receive the Holy Spirit," they do not necessarily mean that believers do not have the Holy Spirit before being baptized in the Holy Spirit. The lack of precision in their language is unfortunate and contributes to misunderstanding about what they teach. Dennis Bennett in *Nine O'Clock in the Morning* clarifies the concept: "Receiving the Holy Spirit or being 'baptized in the Holy Spirit' does not mean getting the Holy Spirit, but 'receiving' or 'making welcome,' permitting the Holy Spirit to fill more areas of our lives and to flow out from us to the world."

TONGUES FOR EVERYONE?

Another controversial question regarding the Holy Spirit involves tongues: may one be filled or baptized in the Holy Spirit without speaking in tongues? That question has always divided Pentecostals and conservative evangelicals.[16] Pentecostal theologican Russell Spittler responds:

As I see it, the Bible gives no direct answer to this question for the reason that nowhere in scripture is the question directly raised. . . .
Luke's concern in Acts, it seems to me, is not to show that speaking in tongues is "initial physical evidence" of the baptism in the Holy Spirit. . . . It is not so much "tongues is the evidence of the Spirit" as it is that "the Spirit is the evidence of being a Christian."[17]

Speaking in tongues as an evidence of baptism or filling is not mentioned in the Epistles or Romans. It is from the book of Acts that Pentecostals base their teaching on the necessity of tongues as evidence of the Spirit's baptism (see 2:4; 10:46; 19:6). Yet there are many instances in Acts where Luke mentions nothing about speaking in tongues as a result of being baptized in the Spirit (see 4:4–42; 8:14–36; 9:1–42; 17:32–34). Russell Spittler further states that "there are thoroughly charismatic churches where glossolalia [tongues] is not viewed as the necessary initial physical evidence of Spirit-baptism. The one who finds himself called to glossolalic levels of encounter with the Holy Spirit by no means is necessarily committed to the theological hardware of the classical Pentecostal churches. The Spirit still blows where he wills."[18]

Yet while tongues are not the focus of the Spirit's filling, spiritual gifts cannot be avoided. Too many evangelicals want the Spirit but not the gifts, an attitude that violates scriptural teaching: "But eagerly desire the greater gifts" (1 Cor. 12:31).

SOCIAL BARRIERS

Unfortunately, legitimate theological questions are not the only obstacles that must be overcome by conservative evangelicals. Social barriers are frequently greater than theological barriers—many who practice the charismatic gifts are immature Christians, persons not formed in mature character. What put me off for years as a pastor was the steady stream of people who, after having been baptized in the Holy Spirit, were now operating with an elitist attitude, telling me that I was not as spiritual as they. Of course, I measured them on the basis of their family life and character—what I think are sound bases for judging growth and maturity of individuals—and I often saw very immature people.

But this was a false basis for judging the validity of spiritual gifts, because the gifts are not given only to *mature* people, they are given to *willing* people. This is not to denigrate the importance of Christian character in the right functioning of the gifts; but we must not confuse immaturity in the exercise of gifts with authenticity of the gifts themselves. It took several years for me to realize that these people had become barriers rather than bridges to my experiencing and understanding the Holy Spirit. When I came to Fuller Seminary I became aware that some of my colleagues spoke in tongues. I recognized in them mature character and life-style.

That Fuller Seminary, the largest evangelical seminary in the world, has Pentecostals on the faculty demonstrates greater understanding between conservative evangelicals and Pentecostals today. Pentecostals are beginning to take conservative evangelicals' concerns more seriously, grappling with tough theological questions and not despising serious theological study as they did earlier in this century. In this regard, the new David du Plessis Center for Christian Spirituality at Fuller Seminary is heartening.

On the part of conservative evangelicals there is change too; strident anti-Pentecostalism, so common only twenty years ago, is receding. Symbolic of this change is Campus Crusade for Christ's recent announcement of change in hiring policy: they now allow Christians who speak in tongues on staff, though they are still not allowed to practice charismatic gifts around other staff members or students. Nevertheless, this is a significant change. Had my friend Scott, whom I wrote about at the beginning of this chapter, been filled with the Holy Spirit today rather than in 1967, Campus Crusade leaders would have affirmed his experience, perhaps resulting in a greater evangelistic harvest. In the least, he might not have remained confused for years about how, as an evangelical, the spiritual gifts operate.[19]

Still, whether we are a conservative evangelical or Pentecostal, the Spirit of Christ, who dwells in us, desires us to express itself through us. It is not enough to acknowledge a theological basis for the practice of the gifts but prefer that no one actually practice them. (To resist the gifts is to resist Christ. This is not only a conservative evangelical problem: a 1979 *Christianity Today* Gallup Poll indicates only seventeen percent of all claiming to be Pentecostals or charismatics in America spoke in tongues, indicating a discrepancy between their belief and practice.)

Tongues, prophecy, words of knowledge—many of the experiences I have described in this book—are an assault on Western Christians' predilection toward personal control of their experience. We find security in the predictable, intellectually understandable experience. In this regard, the Holy Spirit is outside of our control: signs and wonders defy the logic of a scientific worldview.

But there is a sense in which we do control the Holy Spirit. We can always choose to shut it out, to turn away from its leading, to reserve areas of our life for own control. But as we do, these choices affect the very root of our humanity. C. S. Lewis describes how our choices affect us in this way:

I would say that every time you make a choice you are turning the central part of you, the part of you that chooses, into something a little different from what it was before. And taking your life as a whole, with all your innumerable choices, all your life long you are slowly turning this central thing either into a heavenly creature or into a hellish creature: either into a creature that is in harmony with God, and with other creatures, and with itself, or else into one that is in a state of war and hatred with God, and with its fellow-creatures, and with itself.[20]

As Christians, the most fundamental choice that we make is to submit our lives to the control of the Holy Spirit, to ask it to actualize all that it has for us, to release the gifts. If you have never taken this step of faith, you may be filled with the Spirit right now. All that is required is your cooperation in opening your heart to God, asking the Spirit to fill you and take control of your life.

10. What Shall I Do?

In 1981 I was invited to preach at St. Andrew's Anglican Church in Chorleywood, Hertfordshire, England. David Watson and Eddie Gibbs had encouraged Bishop David Pytches, vicar of St. Andrew's, to invite me to speak. He consented, inviting me for two days, a Saturday morning to Sunday evening.

St. Andrew's is a suburban church composed mostly of professionals, including members of the House of Commons, doctors, lawyers, and educators. The pastor before David Pytches had introduced St. Andrew's to the charismatic renewal, which most the members received, though in a fairly subdued fashion. St. Andrew's was and is a "properly Anglican" congregation; I was apprehensive about how the people would respond to teaching about signs and wonders.

Saturday morning I taught about church growth, introducing them to the relationship between the miraculous and growing churches. That evening I spoke on healing, seeing only a moderate response when I prayed over people at the end of the session.

By Sunday morning the church was buzzing about the power of God, some of the people being upset with what I said and did the previous evening. After the Eucharist liturgy, my associates and I again prayed over people. My brother-in-law, Bob Fulton, prayed over a woman who was blind in one eye. When she told Bob what her problem was, he heard her incorrectly, thinking that she had said, "I have arthritis." So he prayed for her to be healed of arthritis (which she didn't have), but the result was her receiving sight. Her response was to begin yelping—something not well received by many in the congregation. Bob almost fainted. By Sunday afternoon David

Pytches's phone was ringing off the hook; people were calling to express concern about what they thought were excesses.

That evening I became concerned about how the congregation was receiving what I had said. But when the evening service began I sensed the powerful presence of the Holy Spirit. Before we left many people were healed and, so it was later reported to me, as many as one hundred young people gave their lives to God that evening or immediately after. Many of them are today preparing for the ministry. To that date, it was the most powerful meeting outside of Vineyard Christian Fellowship gatherings that I had conducted.

David Pytches's response throughout the weekend was joy and laughter, although neither he nor I fully understood what God was doing. As I left Monday morning, his last words, spoken in a mocking dismay, were, "You've torn my church into bits and pieces. What shall I do?"

"What shall I do?" How many times I have heard that question after people have experienced the kingdom of God and tasted the Holy Spirit. When I finish teaching the last session of the course "The Miraculous and Church Growth" at Fuller Seminary, I am often approached by students asking how what I have taught is meant to work in their churches. Over half of my students are pastors or missionaries home on furlough so for them, like for David Pytches, this is a pressing concern.

GO HOME AND BE ONE

Several years ago a Methodist pastor who had recently taken the signs and wonders course at Fuller Seminary wrote me asking for advice. On the verge of retirement, he had initially enrolled in the course to gain credits that would improve his denominational pension. But by the end of the term his life was changed—he had been empowered with the Holy Spirit and it had radically changed his outlook toward the ministry.

"John," he wrote, "I serve on countless committees and do

an endless amount of administration. I want to minister in the power of God, but how can I if I'm always going to district meetings, financial committees, and other sorts of bureaucratic gatherings?"

My advice to him was simple: it does not matter where you are but what you are. Like Jesus, we are called to do the Father's bidding wherever he has placed us. Instead of looking to change things outwardly, I cautioned him, we should let God change us inwardly.

Later I heard back from him. "John," he wrote, "I took your advice. Now I go to committee meetings and ask God to lead me to meet people's needs, to show me what he wants me to say and do. Rarely does a session go by where I do not pray over another pastoral leader or committee member. Further, wherever I go I am always asking the Father to show me his will so I can do his works."

The pastor explained how when he asked folks how they were and they told him their problems, he prayed over them, with excellent results. He did not go into a long explanation with the people about what he was doing, he simply did it.

This is the way most of the members of the Vineyard Christian Fellowship go about their daily lives. One member of our church, Keith Endow, is a realtor who regularly prays over clients who have needs. And they never complain, because the Holy Spirit always comes on them. For example, recently he was showing a client through the home of an elderly couple who were moving due to the recent divorce of a daughter. All around their home were photographs and paintings of their daughter, son-in-law, and grandchildren. The couple was moving to help their daughter through a difficult time. So, just before leaving, Keith told them he was a Christian and asked if he could pray for them. They readily accepted and the Holy Spirit brought a peace and blessing to them.

It is important that we are where God wants us to be. Yet I am convinced that Christians frequently use their situation in life as an excuse for not being used by God right now, that they too often think if only they were in the "right place" they could do the types of things I have described in this book.

DISCIPLES OF JESUS FIRST

Another question people frequently ask is, "Under whom can I get discipled in power evangelism? Who will teach me how to do it?"

I do not discount the need to practical discipleship, the need to learn from older and more experienced brothers and sisters in all areas of Christian living. But when I hear people asking this question, sometimes I wonder if they are bypassing the only true discipler: Jesus. He made the first disciples, and he has continued to make disciples down through the centuries. But too often we allow humans to take his place, missing out on the opportunity to receive his lordship in our heart. We should read good Christian literature, go to conferences, and learn from those who are effective at what I have described in this book, but we should beware of allowing human leaders to take the place of God.

WAITING ON GOD

Finally, we must learn to wait on God, allowing him to speak, act, lead—always yielding our right to control whatever situation that we are in. There is something very simple, almost childlike, about power evangelism. God gives impressions, and we act on them. If he does not speak to us, then we wait—something difficult for action-oriented Western people to do.

This is a simple faith, the kind that Jesus cultivated in the disciples: he always looked for responsive people, men and women who acted on his words, even when they did not understand the words' ramifications (which was often the case). "Come, follow me" was all it took for most of the disciples to leave everything behind and follow the kingdom of God. Our call is no different today.

When the cloudburst of the Holy Spirit came on the disciples at Pentecost, when they were drenched with its power, the key to their success remained the same: emptying themselves from all desire to control God, yielding their lives in service to him.

What should we do? David Pytches stayed at St. Andrew's, not creating radical organizational changes, but encouraging the people to open their hearts to God, walk in his power, and obey his voice. He watched St. Andrew's become a greater source of spiritual renewal and evangelism in the United Kingdom. We might be homemakers, factory workers, secretaries, salespersons, or teachers, but we all have the same challenge as David Pytches and the people of St. Andrew's: to yield control of our lives to the Holy Spirit, learning to hear and do its will, risking all we have to defeat Satan and to advance the kingdom of God.

Appendix A: Signs and Wonders in Church History

Though only a sampling, the following material documents signs and wonders through the centuries. I have limited my sources to major personalities and movements, with a few illustrations of lesser-known people. For further reading and documentation, I refer you to the bibliography.

I separated church history into three ages: patristic, medieval, and Reformation-modern. The twentieth century warrants a separate treatment, found in Appendix B.

THE PATRISTIC ERA, 100–600

JUSTIN MARTYR (ca. 100–165)

Justin was a Christian apologist who had studied all the great philosophies of his day. In his *Second Apology* (ca. 153), Justin, in speaking about the names, meaning, and power of God and Christ, writes concerning exorcism and healing:

For numberless demoniacs throughout the whole world, and in your city, many of our Christian men exorcising them in the name of Jesus Christ, who was crucified under Pontius Pilate, have healed and do heal, rendering helpless and driving the possessing devils out of the men, though they could not be cured by all the other exorcists, and those who used incantations and drugs. (Coxe 6:190).

In his *Dialogue with Trypho* (a learned Jew), Justin refers to the current use of spiritual gifts:

For the prophetical gifts remain with us, even to the present time.

And hence you ought to understand that [the gifts] formerly among your nation have been transferred to us. (Coxe 1:240).

. . . I have already said, and do again say, that it has been prophesied that this would be done by Him after His ascension to heaven. It is accordingly said, "He ascended on high, He led captivity captive, He gave gifts unto the sons of men." And again, in another prophecy, it is said "And it shall come to pass after, I will pour out My Spirit on all flesh, and on My servants, and on My handmaids, and they shall prophesy." Now, it is possible to see amongst us women and men who possess gifts of the Spirit of God . . . " (Coxe 1:243).

IRENAEUS (140–203)

Irenaeus was the bishop of Lyons. His five books *Against Heresies* are devoted to the heresy of Gnosticism. In refuting it he says:

For some do certainly and truly drive out devils, so that those who have thus been cleansed from evil spirits frequently join themselves to the Church. Others have foreknowledge of things to come: they see visions, and utter prophetic expressions. Others still, heal the sick by laying their hands upon them, and they are made whole. Yea, moreover, as I have said, the dead even have been raised up, and remained among us for many years. And what shall I more say? It is not possible to name the number of gifts which the Church, [scattered] throughout the whole world, has received from God, in the name of Jesus Christ.

TERTULLIAN (ca. 160/170–215/220)

Not many details are known concerning Tertullian's life. He was reared in the cultured paganism of Carthage. He became a Christian and joined the Montanist group about 206. He was a prolific writer. In his work *To Scapula*, chapter 5, he gives this account of expelling demons and healing:

All this might be officially brought under your notice, and by the very advocates, who are themselves also under obligations to us, although in court they give their voice as it suits them. The clerk of one of them who was liable to be thrown upon the ground by an evil spirit, was set free from his affliction; and was also the relative of another, and the little boy of a third. How many men of rank (to say nothing of common people) have been delivered from devils, and healed of diseases! Even Severus himself, the father of Antonine, was graciously mindful of the Christians; for he sought out the Christian Proculus, surnamed Torpacion, the steward of Euhodias, and in gratitude for his having once cured him by anointing, he kept him in his palace till the day of his death (Coxe 3:107).

NOVATIAN (210–280)

Novatian of Rome is noted for two reasons: he was the antipope of the puritan party in the church, and he gave the Western church its first full-length treatment of the Trinity. In chapter 29 of *Treatise Concerning the Trinity* he writes of the Spirit:

This is He who places prophets in the Church, instructs teachers, directs tongues, gives powers and healings, does wonderful works, offers discrimination of spirits, affords powers of government, suggests counsels, and orders and arranges whatever other gifts there are of *charismata*; and thus make the Lord's Church everywhere, and in all, perfected and completed (Coxe 5:641).

ANTONY (ca. 251–356)

Our knowledge of Antony depends largely on his biography, written by Athanasius. Chapter 40 of this biography shows Antony's work with the supernatural, especially in dealing with demons:

Once, a very tall demon appeared with a procession of evil spirits and said boldly: "I am the power of God, I am His providence. What do you wish that I grant you?" I then blew my breath at him, calling on the name of Christ, and I tried to strike him. I seemed to have succeeded, for, immediately, vast as he was, he and all his demons disappeared at the name of Christ.

HILARION (ca. 291–371)

Hilarion was an ascetic, educated and converted at Alexandria. By the time he had been in the desert for twenty-two years, he became widely known by reputation throughout the cities of Palestine. Jerome in his *Life of Saint Hilarion* tells of a numbers of the miracles, healings, and expulsions of demons that occurred during his ministry:

Facidia is a small suburb of Rhinocorura, a city of Egypt. From this village, a woman who had been blind for ten years was brought to be blessed by Hilarion. On being presented to him by the brothers (already there were many monks with him), she told him that she had bestowed all her substance on physicians. To her the saint replied: "If what you lost on physicians you had given to the poor, Jesus the true Physician would have healed you." Whereupon she cried aloud and implored him to have mercy on her. Then, following the example of the Saviour, he rubbed spittle upon her eyes and she was immediately cured (15:254–255).

Jerome concludes the section he devoted to telling of Hilarion's life by stating, "There would not be time if I wanted to tell you all the signs and wonders performed by Hilarion . . . " (15:262–263).

MACRINA THE YOUNGER (ca. 328–379/380)

Macrina was the sister of Basil, bishop of Caesarea, and also of Gregory, bishop of Nyssa. Gregory tells of the following healing:

There was with us our little girl who was suffering from an eye ailment resulting from an infectious sickness. It was a terrible and pitiful thing to see her as the membrane around the pupil was swollen and whitened by the disease.

I went to the men's quarters where your brother Peter was Superior, and my wife went to the women's quarters to be with St. Macrina. After an interval of time we were getting ready to leave but the blessed one would not let my wife go, and said she would not give up my daughter, whom she was holding in her arms, until she had given them a meal and offered them "the wealth of philosophy." She kissed the child as one might expect and put her lips on her eyes and, when she noticed the diseased pupil she said, "If you do me the favor of remaining for dinner I will give you a return in keeping with this honor." When the child's mother asked what it was, the great lady replied, "I have some medicine which is especially effective in curing eye disease."

We gladly remained and later started the journey home, bright and happy. Each of us told his own story on the way. My wife was telling everything in order, as if going through a treatise, and when she came to the point at which the medicine was promised, interrupting the narrative, she said, "What have we done? How did we forget the promise, the medicine for the eyes?"

I was annoyed at our thoughtlessness, and quickly sent one of my men back to ask for the medicine, when the child, who happened to be in her nurse's arms, looked at her mother, and the mother, fixing her gaze on the child's eyes said, "Stop being upset by our carelessness." She said this in a loud voice, joyfully and fearfully. "Nothing of what was promised to us has been omitted, but the true medicine that heals diseases, the cure that comes from prayer, this she has given us, and has already worked; nothing at all is left of the disease of the eyes."

As she said this, she took our child and put her in my arms, and I also then comprehended the miracles in the gospel which I had not believed before, and I said, "What a great thing it is for sight to be restored to the blind by the hand of God, if now his handmaiden makes such cures and has done such a thing through faith in him, a fact no less impressive than these miracles."

AMBROSE (ca. 339–397)

Ambrose was the bishop of Milan. When ordained as a bishop his first act was to distribute his wealth among the poor. He was an outstanding preacher and teacher and very outspoken.

Ambrose in *The Holy Spirit (Fathers of the Church)* states that healings and tongues were still given by God:

Behold, the Father established the teachers; Christ also established

them in the churches; and just as the Father gives the grace of healings, so the Son also gives it; just as the Father gives the gift of
tongues, so the Son also has bestowed it (Deferrari 44:150).

AUGUSTINE (354–430)

Augustine was bishop of Hippo and the greatest of the Latin
Fathers. He was baptized by Ambrose in Milan on Easter, 387.
At the close of his life, he wrote *The City of God* (ca. 413–
427). In book 22, chapter 28, Augustine details the miracles
that were occurring in his day: "It is sometimes objected that
the miracles, which Christians claimed to have occurred, no
longer happen." He argues that the ones that happened and
were recorded in the New Testament are "absolutely trustwor-
thy." Then he writes, "The truth is that even today miracles
are being wrought in the name of Christ, sometimes through
His sacraments and sometimes through the intercession of the
relics of his saints."

Augustine then tells of the miracles that happened (Deferrari
24:431–432).

A blind man whose sight was restored (24:433)

The Bishop Innocent of Carthage healed of a rectal fistula
(24:433–437)

Innocentia in Carthage healed of breast cancer (24:437–438)

A doctor in Carthage healed of gout (24:438–439)

An ex-showman of Curcubis healed of paralysis and a hernia
in the scrotum (24:439)

The healing of Hesperius, one of Augustine's neighbors,
whose diseases were caused by "evil spirits" (24:439)

A demonized boy cured, after the demon ripped out his eye
and left it "hanging by a tiny vein as by a root. The pupil
which was black, turned white" (24:440–441)

A young girl in Hippo delivered from demons (24:441)

Florentius of Hippo who prayed for money and received it (24:441–442)

A blind woman healed in Hippo (24:442)

Bishop Lucillus of Synity healed of a fistula (24:442–443)

Eucharius, a Spanish priest, possibly brought back from the dead (24:443)

Martila who was healed and saved (24:443–444)

Three healed of gout (24:444)

A child, who was run over by a cart, healed with no sign of being run over (24:444)

The resuscitation of a nun (24:444)

The resuscitation of a Syrian's daughter (24:444)

Augustine's friend's son who was raised from the dead (24:445)

Augustine ends his narrative of miracles by telling his readers that there are too many miracles to list. "It is a simple fact," Augustine writes, "that there is no lack of miracles even in our day. And the God who works the miracles we read of in the scriptures uses any means and manner he chooses."

GREGORY OF TOURS (ca. 538–594)

Gregory was a bishop and historian. He was a prolific writer, whose works provide invaluable knowledge of sixth-century church life (Douglas 1974, 436). There are many accounts of healings that occurred in Gregory's time. They are to be found in his *Dialogues*, where he also relates the expelling of a demon and his own healing:

Eleutherius, whom I mentioned previously, abbot of the Monastery of St. Mark, the Evangelist adjoining the walls of Spoleto, lived with me for a long time in my monastery at Rome and died there. His disciples say that he raised a dead person to life by the power of his prayer. He was well known for his simplicity and compunction of heart, and undoubtedly through his tears this humble, childlike soul obtained many favors from almighty God.

I will tell you about a miracle of his which I had him describe to me in his own simple words. Once while he was traveling, evening came on before he could find a lodging for the night, so he stopped at a convent. There was a little boy in this convent who was troubled every night by an evil spirit. So, after welcoming the man of God to their convent, the nuns asked him to keep the boy with him that night. He agreed, and allowed the boy to rest near him. In the morning the nuns asked him with deep concern whether he had done anything for the boy. Rather surprised that they should ask, he said, "No." Then they acquainted him with the boy's condition, informing him that not a night passed without the evil spirit troubling the boy. Would Eleutherius please take him along to the monastery because they could no longer bear to see him suffer. The man of God agreed to do so.

The boy remained a long time in the monastery without being troubled in the least. Highly pleased at this, the old abbot allowed his joy at the boy's healthy condition to exceed moderation. "Brothers," he said to his monks, "the Devil had his joke with the sisters, but once he encountered real servants of God, he no longer dared to come near this boy." That every instant, hardly waiting for Eleutherius to finish speaking, the Devil again took possession of the young boy, tormenting him in the presence of all. The sight of it filled the old man's heart with grief, and when his monks tried to console him he said, "Upon my word! Not one of you shall taste bread today until this boy is snatched out of the Devil's power."

He prostated himself in prayer with all his monks and continued praying until the boy was freed from the power of the evil spirit. The cure was complete and the Devil did not dare molest him any further.

GREGORY I (THE GREAT) (540–604)

Gregory the Great was pope from 590 to 604. His *Dialogues* (593–94) were described by the author himself as stories of "the miracles of the Fathers which were done in Italy." The *Dialogues* contain supernatural tales, which divide neatly into three classes: stories of visions, stories of prophecies, and stories of miracles.

The following, a summary of one of Gregory's stories, is taken from Frederick Dudden's seminal work on the life of Gregory:

One day at Subiaco, the little monk Placidus, the future Apostle of his [Gregory's] Order in Sicily, went to the lake to draw water, but overbalanced himself and fell in. Benedict, who was sitting in his cell, was supernaturally aware of the occurrence, and cried out hastily to his disciple Maurus: "Run, Brother Maurus, for the child who went to fetch water has fallen into the lake, and the stream has carried him a great way." Maurus ran down to the edge of the lake, and then, "thinking still that he went on dry land, he ran on the water," caught the drifting boy by the hair and brought him safely back. It was only when he stood again on the firm ground that Maurus realized that a miracle had taken place, and "much astonished, he wondered how he had done that which knowingly he would not have dared to venture." (Dudden, vol. 1, 1905, 334).

THE MEDIEVAL ERA, 600–1500

ST. FRANCIS OF ASSISI (1181–1226)

St. Francis was the founder of the Franciscan order. He had an extensive healing ministry. The following selections are taken from a vast number of miracles that occurred in the ministry of Francis:

Once when the holy man of God Francis was going about through various regions to preach the kingdom of God, he came to a certain city called Toscanella. There, when he was sowing the seed of life in his usual way, a certain soldier of that city gave him hospitality; he had an only son who was lame and weak of body. Though he was a young child, he had passed the years of weaning; still he remained in a cradle. When the father of the boy saw the great sanctity of the man of God, he humbly cast himself at his feet, begging from him health for his son. But Francis, who considered himself useless and unworthy of such great power and grace, refused for a long time to do this. But finally overcome by the insistence of his petitions, he prayed and then put his hand upon the boy and, blessing him, raised him up. Immediately, with all present looking on and rejoicing, the boy arose completely restored and began to walk here and there about the house.

Once when the man of God Francis had come to Narni and was staying there for a number of days, a certain man of that city, Peter by name, lay in bed paralyzed. For a period of five months he had been so deprived of the use of all his limbs that he could not rise at all or move himself even a little; and thus having completely lost the use of his feet and hands and head, he could only move his tongue and open his eyes. When he heard that Francis had come to Narni, he sent a messenger to the bishop of that city to ask him for the love of God to send the servant of the most high God to him, confident that he would be freed from the illness from which he suffered at the sight and presence of Francis. And so it happened that, when the blessed Francis had come to him and had made the sign of the cross over him from his head to his feet, he was immediately healed and restored to his former health. (Hermann n.d., 59–60).

WALDENSIAN COMMUNITY

This was a movement in the Middle Ages whose characteristics included evangelical obedience to the gospel, rigorous asceticism, aversion to recognizing the ministry of unworthy priests, belief in visions, prophecies, and spirit possession (Douglas 1974, 1026). A. J. Gordon in his book *The Ministry of Healing* quotes the following doctrine of the Waldensians:

Therefore, concerning this anointing of the sick, we hold it *as an article of faith,* and profess sincerely from the heart that sick persons, when they ask it, may lawfully be anointed with the anointing oil by one who joins them in praying that it may be efficacious to the healing of the body according to the design and end and effect mentioned by the apostles; and we profess that such an anointing performed according to the apostolic design and practice will be healing and profitable (Gordon 1802, 65).

VINCENT FERRER (1350–1419)

Vincent was a Dominican preacher who was born in Valencia. Known as the "Angel of the Judgment," he preached across Europe for almost twenty years. The *New Catholic Encyclopedia* records the following:

Vincent was disillusioned; he became gravely ill. In a vision, he was commissioned by the Lord, who was accompanied by St. Dominic and St. Francis, "to go through the world preaching Christ." After a year had passed Benedict permitted him to go. In November 1399, therefore, he set forth from Avignon and spent 20 years in apostolic preaching. As the spirit moved him or as he was requested, he visited and revisited places throughout Spain, southern France, Lombardy, Switzerland, northern France, and the Low Countries. With fiery eloquence he preached the need of repentance and the coming of the Judgment. He seldom remained in any one place for more than a day, and then only when the people had been long neglected or when heresy or paganism was rife. Miracles in the order of nature and of grace accompanied his steps (14:681).

The *Catholic Encyclopedia Dictionary* also notes: "He is said by some to have had the gift of tongues . . . " (1002).

COLETTE OF CORBI (d. 1447)

The following is recorded about Colette in *The Lives of the Saints*:

In 1410, she founded a covenant at Besancon; in 1415, she introduced a reform into the convent of the Cordeliers, at Dole, and in succession into nearly all the convents in Lorraine, Champagne, and Picardy. In 1416, she founded a house of her order at Poligny, at the foot of the Jura, and another at Auxonne. "I am dying of curiosity to see this wonderful Colette, who resuscitates the dead," wrote the Duchess of Bourbon, about this time. For the fame of the miracles and labours of the carpenter's daughter was in every mouth (Baring-Gould 1897, 3:99–100).

THE REFORMATION AND THE MODERN ERA, 1500–1900

MARTIN LUTHER (1483–1546)

In *Luther: Letters of Spiritual Council*, the following letter of Martin Luther is recorded:

The tax collector in Torgau and the councilor in Belgern have written me to ask that I offer some good advice and help for Mrs. John Korner's afflicted husband. I know of no worldly help to give. If the physicians are at a loss to find a remedy, you may be sure that it is not a case of ordinary melancholy. It must, rather, be an affliction that comes from the devil, and this must be counteracted by the power of Christ with the prayer of faith. This is what we do, and what we have been accustomed to do, for a cabinet maker here was similarly afflicted with madness and we cured him by prayer in Christ's name.

Accordingly you should proceed as follows: Go to him with the deacon and two or three good men. Confident that you, as pastor of the place, are clothed with the authority of the ministerial office, lay your hands upon him and say, "Peace be with you, dear brother, from God our Father and from our Lord Jesus Christ." Thereupon repeat the Creed and the Lord's Prayer over him in a clear voice, and close with these words: "O God, almighty Father, who has told us through thy Son, 'Verily, verily I say unto you, Whatsoever ye shall ask the Father in my name, he will give it you'; who has commanded and encouraged us to pray in his name, 'Ask, and ye shall receive,' and who in like manner hast said, 'Call upon me in the day of trouble: I will deliver thee, and thou shalt glorify me'; we unworthy sinners, relying on these thy words and commands, pray for thy mercy with such faith as we can muster. Graciously deign to free this man from all evil, and put to nought the work that Satan has done in him, to the honor of thy name and the strengthening of the faith of believers; through the same Jesus Christ, thy Son, our Lord, who liveth and reigneth with thee, world without end. Amen." Then, when you depart, lay your hands upon the man again and say, "These signs shall follow them that believe; they shall lay hands on the sick, and they shall recover." Do this three times, once on each of three successive days. (Tappert n.d., 18:52).

In *Luther's Works*, concerning prophecy he says, "If you wish to prophesy, do it in such a way that it does not go beyond faith so that your prophesying can be in harmony with the peculiar quality of faith." He goes on to write that "one may prophesy new things but not things that go beyond the bounds of faith . . ." (Oswald n.d., 25:444–451).

IGNATIUS OF LOYOLA (1491–1556)

Ignatius was the founder of the Society of Jesus. He was wounded in the Spanish army in 1521. While recuperating he read the *Life of Christ* by Ludolph of Saxony. This inspired him to become a "soldier" for Christ. He entered a monastery and spent nearly a year at ascetic practices. Here he composed the essence of *Spiritual Exercises*. In them he writes the following about the Spirit:

The Spirit of God breathes where he will; he does not ask our permission; he meets us on his own terms and distributes his charisms as He pleases. Therefore, we must always be awake and ready; we must be pliable so that he can use us in new enterprises. We cannot lay down the law to the Spirit of God! He is only present with his gifts where he knows that they are joined with the multiplicity of charisms in the one Church. All the gifts of this church stem from one source—God. What Paul says in the twelfth chapter of his First Epistle to the Corinthians is still true today! This should give us the strength to overcome every form of clerical jealousy, mutual suspicion, power-grabbing, and the refusal to let others—who have their own gifts of the Spirit—go on their own way. That is what the Spirit wants from us! He is not so narrow-minded as we sometimes are with our recipes! He can lead to himself in different ways, and He wants to direct the church through a multiplicity of functions, offices, and gifts. The church is not supposed to be a military academy in which everything is uniform, but she is supposed to be the body of Christ in which he, the one spirit, exerts his power in all the members. Each one of these members proves that he really is a member of this body by letting the other members be. (Rahner 1962, 254–255).

TERESA OF AVILA (1515–1582)

Teresa, a Carmelite reformer, mystic, and writer, was born in Spain and educated by Augustinian nuns. In her autobiography there are frequent accounts of the ecstasy she experienced from God. In it she writes, "What I say about not ascending to God unless he raises one up is language of the Spirit. He who has had some experience will understand me, for I don't know how to describe this being raised up if it isn't understood through experience" (12:5). She refers to this kind of speech again when talking about prayer (16:1–2):

I don't know any other terms for describing it or how to explain it. Nor does the soul then know what to do because it doesn't know whether to speak or to be silent, whether to laugh or to weep. This prayer is a glorious foolishness, a heavenly madness where the true wisdom is learned; and it is for the soul a most delightful way of enjoying. In fact five or even six years ago the Lord often gave me this prayer in abundance, and I didn't understand it; nor did I know how to speak of it.

VALENTINE GREATLAKES (d. 1638)

David Robertson writes in his article "From Epidauros to Lourdes: A History of Healing by Faith" about an Irishman named Greatlakes:

He was a Protestant in Catholic Ireland and fled to England in 1641 at the outbreak of the Irish Rebellion. For a time he served under Cromwell. In 1661, after a period of depression, he came to believe that God had given him, a mere commoner, the power to cure scrofula. When he began trying to cure the king's evil, his friends and acquaintances were astounded to find that he did indeed seem able to produce a regression in this disease. This stunning achievement led him to try his hand at other illnesses like epilepsy, paralysis, deafness, ulcers, and diverse nervous disorders, and he found that his touch was efficacious in these cases as well. Soon word of his uncanny ability spread far and wide and he was besieged by multitudes of sick people. The crowds that came to him were so great that he could not accommodate all of them even if he worked from 6:00 in the morning until 6:00 at night (Frazier 1973, 187).

THE QUAKERS, OR THE SOCIETY OF FRIENDS (1640–present)

The Quakers' origins are traced back to English Puritanism in the 1640s. The first leader was George Fox, who preached a message of the New Age of the Spirit. They were opposed by both the Puritans and Anglicans. The typical Quaker meeting was characterized by the people waiting for the Spirit to speak through them and by the people "quaking" as God moved among them. The following are some excerpts from Fox's *Journal*:

In the year 1648, as I was sitting in a friend's house in Nottinghamshire (for by this time the power of God had opened the hearts of some to receive the word of life and reconciliation), I saw there was a great crack to go throughout the earth, and a great smoke to go as the crack went; and that after the crack there should be a great shaking: this was the earth in people's hearts, which was to be shaken before the seed of God was raised out of the earth. And it was so: for the Lord's power began to shake them and great meetings we begun to have, and mighty power and work of God there was amongst people, to the astonishment of both people and priests (Fox 1901, 23).

THE HUGUENOTS (Formally organized in 1559)

Huguenots was a nickname for the French Calvinists. Henry Baird writes in his book *The Huguenots* the following concerning some of the phenomena of this religious group:

Respecting the physical manifestations, there is little discrepancy between the accounts of friend and foe. The persons affected were men and women, the old and the young. Very many were children, boys and girls of nine or ten years of age. They were sprung from the people—their enemies said, from the dregs of the people—ignorant and uncultured; for the most part unable to read or write, and speaking in everyday life the *patois* of the province with which alone they were conversant. Such persons would suddenly fall backward, and, while extended at full length on the ground, undergo strange and apparently involuntary contortions; their chests would seem to heave, their stomachs to inflate. On coming gradually out of this condition, they appeared instantly to regain the power of speech. Beginning often in a voice interrupted by sobs, they soon poured forth a torrent of words—cries for mercy, calls to repentance, exhortations to the bystanders to cease frequenting the mass, denunciations of the church of Rome, prophecies of coming judgment. From the mouths of those that were little more than babes came texts of Scripture, and discourse in good and intelligible French, such as they never used in their conscious hours. When the trance ceased, they declared that they remembered nothing of what had occurred, or of what they had said. In rare cases they retained a general and vague impression, but nothing more. There was no appearance of deceit or collusion, and no indication that in uttering their predictions respecting coming events they had any thought of prudence, or doubt as to the truth of what they foretold. Brueys, their most inveterate opponent, is no less positive on this point than are the witnesses who are most favorable to them. "These poor madmen," he said, "believed that they were indeed inspired by the Holy Ghost. They prophesied without any (ulterior) design, without evil intent, and with so little reserve, that they always boldly marked the day, the place and persons of whom they spoke in their predictions" (2:186–187).

THE JANSENISTS (ca. 1731)

"The expectation of miracles and other supernatural signs had become almost an integral part of the Jansenist worldview by the end of the seventeenth century," writes Robert Kreiser in his book *Miracles, Convulsions, and Ecclesiastical Politics in Early Eighteenth Century Paris*. One such miracle that he records is the cure of Pascal's niece in March 1656. Marguerite had been suffering for a long time from a serious and disfiguring lachrymal fistula in the corner of her eye. She was healed when a holy thorn was simply touched to her eye. The miracle was supported by substantial medical evidence and made a profound impression on the public.

JOHN WESLEY (1703–1791)

John Wesley was the founder of the Methodist church. In his *Journal* he writes:

Wed., Aug. 15, 1750—By reflecting on an odd book which I had read in this journey, *The General Delusion of Christians with Regard to Prophecy*, I was fully convinced of what I had once suspected: (1) That the Montanists, in the second and third centuries, were real, scriptural Christians; and (2) That the grand reason why the miraculous gifts were so soon withdrawn, was not only that faith and holiness were wellnigh lost, but that dry, formal, orthodox men began even then to ridicule whatever gifts they had not themselves, and to decry them all as either madness or imposture.

Wesley wrote a letter to Thomas Church in June 1746 in which he states:

Yet I do not know that God hath anyway precluded himself from thus exerting His sovereign power from working miracles in any kind or degree in any age to the end of the world. I do not recollect any scripture wherein we are taught that miracles were to be confined within the limits either of the apostolic or the Cyprianic age, or of any period of time, longer or shorter, even till the restitution of all things. I have not observed, either in the Old Testament, or the New, any intimation at all of this kind. St. Paul says, indeed, once, concerning two of the miraculous gifts of the Spirit (so, I think, that test is usually understood), "Whether there be prophecies, they shall fail; whether there be tongues, they shall cease." But he does not say, either that these or any other miracles shall cease till faith and hope shall cease also, till they all be swallowed up in the vision of God, and love be all in all (Telford n.d., 2:261).

AZUSA STREET (1906)

In 1905, Charles Parham moved his school from Topeka, Kansas, to Houston, Texas. There William J. Seymour, a black evangelist, joined the school. He embraced the "teaching on tongues" but did not experience this in Houston. In 1906, Seymour was invited to speak in a small black Nazarene church in Los Angeles. On April 1, 1906, Seymour spoke in tongues. The small group soon outgrew the little house on Bonnie Brae and moved into an old livery stable at 312 Azusa Street. Seymour was the central figure of the Azusa Street revival. The revival continued for three and a half years at Azusa Street. Services were held three times daily—morning, afternoon, and evening. Speaking in tongues was a central attraction, but healing of the sick was not far behind. Seymour was the pastor of the congregation, which was made up of both blacks and whites, until his death in 1929. Pilgrims to Azusa were common and came from all parts of the world, according to Frank Bartleman in *Azusa Street* (136).

Appendix B: Signs and Wonders in the Twentieth Century

Signs and wonders are still occurring in this century, both apart from and under the immediate supervision of Western denominations. Indications are that churches grow most rapidly where Western Christians—and their antisupernatural bent—have the least immediate influence.

The following are random case studies gathered by myself and others. I only recount examples that demonstrate the relationship between signs and wonders and church growth.

SOUTH AFRICA

In South Africa there is an Indian community of about eight hundred thousand that was solidly opposed to the Christian faith. Very few Indians became Christians. About twenty or twenty-five years ago, through a series of healing campaigns, two Pentecostal denominations began to grow among the Indians. One of those Pentecostal churches is now twenty-five thousand strong, the other fifteen thousand.[1]

REINHARD BONNKE

Bonnke is a German missionary ministering through an independent organization called Christ for All Nations mainly in the black homelands of South Africa. His first campaign was conducted in Gaberones, Botswana, with the Apostolic

Faith Mission (A.F.M.) that at that time had only forty members in the city. Nightly after preaching, Bonnke would be joined by Richard Ngidi to pray for the sick. After only six days they were attracting crowds of two thousand to an auditorium that seated eight hundred. Dramatic healings resulted and the meetings were moved to a stadium where they attracted a nightly audience of ten thousand people.

The next campaign was held in Sibasa, northern Transvaal. Within seven days after the occurrence of extraordinary miracles, the stadium was filled with a nightly audience of thirty thousand people despite heavy rains. In 1979, Bonnke held a campaign for the A.F.M. in Bloemfontein, South Africa. Hundreds were saved, healed, and baptized in water. After a campaign of twenty days they established a new church with a baptized membership of over six hundred people. Christ for All Nations has now built a tent that accommodates thirty-four thousand people and is using it regularly.[2]

ERLO STEGEN

Stegen is a German missionary working with the Zulus in Kwasizabantu in South Africa. The first twelve years of his ministry in their region were completely unsuccessful. At that point, totally frustrated, Stegen began a detailed study of the book of Acts with a group of black associates. They identified signs and wonders as being the key to the rapid growth of the early church. Later they experienced the filling of the Holy Spirit. The details of that experience were described as being similar to the account in Acts 2.

Immediately after leaving the room where they had experienced the anointing of the Holy Spirit, Stegen and the group were met by a demon-possessed woman who said, "Something just drove me to come here and ask you to pray for me." They cast the demon out and the woman was delivered and set free. The woman returned to her village and caused a small revival. She preached the gosel, prayed for the sick, and hundreds gave their lives to the Lord.

From that point on people began streaming to Kwasizabantu. Those who were healed, saved, and filled with the Spirit went back to his or her own village and proclaimed the gospel there. This was the start of a large revival.[3]

IVORY COAST

PROPHET HARRIS

The prophet William Wade Harris, a Liberian of the Berbos tribe, grew up under the influence of Christianity. His uncle was a Methodist preacher in Liberia. At the age of twenty, Harris had a deep religious experience. However, his Christian ministry did not begin until he was sixty years old.

In 1913, "Prophet Harris," as he was called, entered the Ivory Coast to embark on one of the greatest evangelistic tours ever recorded in African history. Rene Bureau in his unpublished dissertation "The Prophet Harris" adds some insight on the way God called Prophet Harris to become a missionary. He reveals the testimony given to a Catholic priest in the Ivory Coast before Harris started his journey along the coast:

I am a prophet of God. Four years ago I was awakened at night. I saw my guardian angel under my bed. He hit me three times on the forehead, saying, "I am going to take your wife from you. She will die, but I will give you many people to help you. Before your wife dies, she will give you six shillings, that will be your fortune. You will never need anything. I will be with you always and reveal to you the mission of God." That's why I have come. I am here to do God's mission.

William Harris then began his journey along the coastline of the Ivory Coast. He dressed in a white robe and turban, carried a Bible, a bamboo cross, and gourd of water. He went everywhere proclaiming the message of salvation in Christ. He never read from the Bible, because the people were illiterate, but he quoted from memory passages dealing with salvation. He taught songs and proclaimed that worship of fetishes and idols was wrong and God would punish people who practiced such things. He challenged the people to burn their fetishes and follow God.

Harris would invite those wanting to follow God to come forward and kneel before the cross. They would come and place both hands on the bamboo cross, confessing their sins. Harris would then touch the tops of their heads with his Bible. The new converts would tremble, and Harris would expel demons.

In Jackville, Harris healed the chief's wife, who was dying. He said, "Touch this cross, get up, and walk." She did, and the entire village was converted.

He organized groups of believers and advised them to construct chapels. He placed a pastor in charge of each and had each group select twelve apostles to direct the church. Some converts were sent to the interior tribes to bring them the message of salvation. Harris told these newly formed congregations that missionaries would come to explain the Bible.

After two years of ministry in the Ivory Coast, Harris was arrested by the French authorities and sent back to Liberia. The French feared this new religious movement and attempted to stop it.[4]

JACQUES GIRAUD

The church in the Ivory Coast was typical of the church in many countries of Asia, Africa, and Latin America. The Ivory Coast has about four million people, with the Roman Catholic Church claiming about thirty thousand. The Methodist Church dates from 1924 and has sixty thousand. Seven small Protestant denominations, with a total baptized membership of about eleven thousand, have arisen because of the faithful work of missionaries. Their growth rate is seventy percent per decade. (About a hundred and fifty dedicated missionaries from America, Switzerland, and France are helping these churches and are doing a multitude of good deeds.)

Pastor Jacques Giraud, a French missionary to the West Indies, arrived in the Ivory Coast in March 1973 to dedicate an Assemblies of God church building in Abidjan. As the meetings progressed, people began to be healed. The crowds grew and the meetings were moved to the stadium. Truckloads of people came from all parts of the Ivory Coast. The papers and radio stations reported the events. Leading government officials and their wives flocked to the stadium.

Pastor Giraud would tell about one of Christ's miracles and preach for an hour on God's almighty power to heal. Then he would say, "I don't heal. God heals. I ask him to release his power. Put your hand where it hurts and join me in prayer." He would pour out his heart in believing prayer to God for healing. After a half hour of prayer he would invite those God had healed to come to the front. Crutches were thrown away. Bent and arthritic persons stood erect. Blind men walked forward seeing. Scores and sometimes hundreds came. God had given them at least a measure of healing. (Thousands were also not healed.)

Although he was a minister of the Assemblies of God denomination, it was his practice to direct converts to the local churches and missions for shepherding. At Toumoudi he had the Christian and Missionary Alliance missionaries and ministers on the platform with him. He said to the people, "When you place your faith in Jesus Christ, call these men to baptize you and shepherd you."

Reverend Fred Pilding, a missionary of the Christian and Missionary Alliance working in the Ivory Coast, fills in some details in the *Alliance Witness*, September 26, 1973:

The crusade began in Bouake on June 18th and continued for three weeks. Morning attendance averaged about 4,000. From 6,000 to 15,000 turned out in the evenings with a high of 25,000 one Sunday. The sick were seated on the grass on the playing field, and all the others occupied the grandstands. As the evangelist presented Jesus Christ, the same yesterday, today, and forever, people became aware of his continuing power today, through a healing receptive place. It became easier for them to trust him as Savior.

A hunchback came to the meeting, groveling in the dirt, under the influence of demons. The demons were exorcised in the name of Jesus and he was instantly healed. The next day he attended the meetings nicely dressed, perfectly calm, and gave his testimony.

Whenever those who were healed testified, witnesses were asked to verify each healing. Pastor Giraud again and again cited Mark 16:15–18 as every believer's commission and emphasized that in Christ's name they were to cast out devils and lay hands on the sick and they shall recover. He refuted vigorously the title of healer. His ministry, he said, was to inspire faith in the gospel. "It is in the name of Jesus that people are healed."

After the Toumoudi meeting, groups of converts from 81 villages around Toumoudi sought out the Alliance missionaries and ministers, begging them to come and make them Christians. After the Bouake meeting, responses were received from over 100 villages. A hundred and forty cards were filled out from one small town alone.

From one village near Bouake 10 cards had been received. The missionary went to visit this village. Seeing him, one of the men who had been healed rushed off to get some of the pagan village elders. While waiting, the missionary said to the children, "Do you know Pastor Giraud's song?" Immediately they broke into joyful singing, "Up, up with Jesus, down, down with Satan, Alleluia!" People came pouring out and the missionary preached and then asked, "How many will follow God and leave their old ways?" More than half immediately said, "We will." In another village the Chief said, "Fetish is dead, we shall all become Christians."

The pastors and missionaries were faced with great opportunities. The challenge was to take advantage of this enthusiasm, which could dissipate rapidly, and channel these people into ongoing responsible churches of Christians who know the Lord, obey his word. Nothing like this had happened in their experience on the Ivory Coast, and they were naturally fearful, lest the excitement prove transient as it very well might.[5]

ARGENTINA

TOMMY HICKS

In 1952, God spoke to American evangelist Tommy Hicks through a vision, telling him to go to South America and preach the gospel. In 1954, while on his way to Buenos Aires, the name Peron flashed into Hick's mind. He knew nobody by that name. Near the flight's destination he asked the flight attendant whether she knew anybody by that name. She replied, "Yes, Mr. Peron is the president of Argentina." Hicks sought an appointment with Mr. Peron but ran into difficulties. Then an extraordinary event took place at the president's office. While seeking an interview, Hicks encountered Mr. Peron's secretary, who had a bad leg. Hicks prayed for him and he was instantly healed. This resulted in Hicks being introduced to General Peron.

Peron received Hicks warmly and instructed his assistant to give Hicks whatever he asked for. On Hicks's request, a large stadium was made available to him as well as free access to the government controlled radio and press. The campaign lasted for fifty-two days. Hicks preached the gospel on the saving power of Jesus, emphasizing divine dealing. Over two million people attended the meetings. Some two hundred thousand people attended the campaign on the final night. Although almost all the local churches grew as a result of the campaign, the Assemblies of God gained the most. Their growth, from 174 in 1951 to nearly two thousand members in 1956, reflects the tremendous impact of Hicks's campaign.[6]

INDIA

Suba Rao was the headmaster of a government school in India, a member of one of the middle castes and a wealthy man. He hated missionaries and laughed at baptism. He thought of the church as an assembly of the low castes (which in India it was).

One of his near neighbors and close friends fell sick. He was sick for two years and was gradually wasting away. He went to many doctors, to no avail. One night, while Suba Rao was asleep, the Lord Jesus appeared to him and said, "If you will go and lay your hand on that man's head and pray in my name, I will heal him." Suba Rao woke up and laughed; he thought it was a funny dream and went back to sleep.

The next night the Lord Jesus stood by his side and said, "If you go and lay your hand on that man's head and pray for him to be healed, I will heal him." Suba Rao woke up. He didn't laugh this time, and he didn't go back to sleep; but he didn't lay his hands on the sick man either. He thought, "That's impossible!" The third night the Lord Jesus appeared to him again. This time he got up at once and went to his neighbor. He laid his hand on the man's head, prayed for him, and in the morning the man said, "I feel much better. Do it again." The man was healed.

Suba Rao threw out his idols. He started to read the Bible. He started a Bible study class among his neighbors. Still today he ridicules baptism. He has still not joined any church, but he proclaims himself a follower of the Lord Jesus. The healing of people in Jesus' name has become his chief occupation. Joining the church, which in India is composed largely of the lowest castes of Indian society is, he thinks, an impossible step for him. Still, the Lord Jesus heals men through Suba Rao.[7]

THE NISHI TRIBALS

The Nishi Tribals in Sulansini Division in India are now receptive to the miraculous. It all started when a high government official's youngest son fell terminally ill:

A Hindu pharmacist, recognizing that the child was beyond medical help, advised that the father "Try the Christian God, Jesus Christ. I have once heard that he had raised a man called Lazarus, who had already been dead for three days!" As the father approached his house, he heard crying and wailing, and he knew that his son must have died. He went into the house, discovered that it was so, but then went into the son's room, placed his hand on the chest of his dead son and prayed, "Jesus, I do not know who you are, but I have just heard that you raised Lazarus from the dead after three days. My son has died only a few hours ago, and if you raise him up, I promise you, even though I do not know who you are, my family and I will worship you." Immediately the eyes of the child began to flicker again and he was restored to life. The impact of the miracle was tremendous. The people cried, "Jesus, who are you? What love you have for us!" Within the next couple of weeks, hundreds gave their lives to Jesus.[8]

CHINA

David Wang is the general director of Asian Outreach. He visits mainland China quite often and has regular contact with the believers there. His reports of what the Lord is doing in China are very exciting.

For example, he tells us that near Foochon, there is a place called Christian Mountain. The community of Christian Mountain consists of between thirty and fifty thousand people, of whom ninety percent are Christians. The growth of this Christian community can be related directly to the deliverance of a girl possessed by demons in 1969–1970.

INDONESIA

The well-known German theologian Kurt Koch did some excellent research on what is now called the "revival in Indonesia." Timor is one of the islands at the eastern extremity of Indonesia. Out of a population of one million, some four hundred and fifty thousand people belong to the former Dutch Reformed Church. According to Koch, by the early sixties the spiritual state of the churches was almost catastrophic. Timor had never been evangelized; only "Christianized." In 1964, God instructed a man named Jephtah (a teacher on the island of Rote) in a vision to travel to Timor and hold a healing campaign there. From the start of the campaign God confirmed Jephtah's calling with a mighty ministry of signs and wonders. Following the close of the campaign, a further week of healing was held in Sol. According to various reports, which were later confirmed, several thousand people were healed. All of this was the start of what developed into a mighty revival, with thousands being saved. In one area an evangelistic team won more than nine thousand people for Christ in just two weeks.

CANADA

RED SUCKER LAKE, MANITOBA, 1951

A young couple, new missionaries, were spending their first winter of marriage in an isolated Cree Indian village near Red Sucker Lake. It was toward springtime, and lakes and rivers were clogged with ice, making float flying (landing airplanes on lakes) impossible. There was neither telephone nor radio communication to the outside.

The missionaries were in the initial stages of learning the Indian language. The small child of a prominent native became very seriously ill. There were no medical facilities in the village and the workers had no medical training. As the child worsened, friends suggested that perhaps one of the new missionaries would pray for the child. The child's father refused, saying, "He's a false teacher, how could he do any good?" The days passed and the child's condition became critical until it was clear to all he was dying. The neighbors said, "Well, it can't hurt now to let him pray for him. The child's dying anyway." The father reluctantly yielded. The missionary came to the tent, prayed briefly for the child to get well, then left. The next day the child had completely recovered. Today, the grown child is living a normal life, happily married. Eventually the father was converted, went to Bible school, and became the pastor of the Indian church in the village.[9]

Notes

CHAPTER 1

1. James Kallas, *Jesus and the Power of Satan* (Philadelphia: Westminster, 1968), 119–21.
2. It is not my intention to equate the fifteen books of the Apocrypha with canon. In Article VI of the Thirty-Nine Articles of the Church of England, we read:

   And the other Books (as Hierome [Jerome] saith) the Church doth read for example of life and instruction of manners; but yet doth it not apply them to establish any doctrine.

3. The Hebrew understanding of time was different from that of the Greeks. For the Hebrews, God's purpose moves to a consummation (this is called a linear view of time). By contrast, the cyclical view of time was common in the ancient world, a view in which events just go on or return to the point whence they began, with no sense of purpose or direction. The New Testament Greek words that we translate eternity (*eis ton aiona*, usually translated "forever") literally means "for ages" (also see Mark 3:29; Luke 1:33, 55; Gal. 1:5; 1 Pet. 4:11; Rev. 1:18). The Hebrew concept of time emphasized the times appointed by God to fulfill his purposes on earth. Finally, the Hebrews divided history into two stages. The first, this age, is evil; the second, the age to come, is good.
4. The Pseudephigrapha are those Jewish writings that were excluded from the Old Testament canon and that find no place in the Apocrypha.
5. George Ladd, *A Theology of the New Testament* (Grand Rapids, MI: Eerdmans, 1974), 48.
6. Ibid., 69.
7. I do not imply that Satan is equal in power to Christ. Any authority that Satan has is derived from God. For a time, God has permitted Satan to afflict the world so Christ's mercy and judgment can be demonstrated in the creation, especially in his work on the cross.
8. The terms "kingdom of heaven" and "kingdom of God" are used interchangeably in the New Testament.
9. The Greek word used in New Testament for "church," *ekklesia*, was also used in the Greek translation of the Old Testament (the Septuagint). It

literally means "the called out ones," again indicating that the New Testament church stands in direct continuity with the Old Testament people of God.

10. Ladd, *A Theology of the New Testament*, 118.
11. Ibid.
12. For greater depth on the subject of this entire section, see Ladd, *A Theology of the New Testament*, 111–19.
13. Much of this chapter is based on material gleaned from the writings of George Ladd and James Kallas. For those readers interested in further reading on the kingdom of God, I recommend Ladd's *A Theology of the New Testament* and Kallas's *The Real Satan* (Minneapolis, MN: Augsburg, 1975). For a view similar to Ladd's, Catholic readers may refer to Rudolf Schnackenburg's *The Moral Teaching of the New Testament* (New York: Seabury, 1965), especially chap. 1. Schnackenburg fits Jesus' moral demands "principally (though not exclusively) within the framework of his gospel of the reign of God" (p. 13).
14. Jesus came into the world to save men and women from Satan, to forgive and regenerate us, to offer eternal life to all who believe in him. The focus of this book is signs and wonders for the purpose of overcoming Satan's kingdom and as an avenue for leading many to Christ. By focusing on signs and wonders I imply neither that they are the totality of our salvation, nor that the analogy of the church as an army is the only way to understand it. We are also called a family, a refuge, a people, a nation, and so on, each connoting different aspects of God's purpose in salvation.
15. Kallas, *The Real Satan*, 60.
16. George Ladd, *The Presence of the Future* (Grand Rapids, MI: Eerdmans, 1974), 160–61.
17. Ibid., 162.

CHAPTER 2

1. Many questions about demonization are raised in this illustration and throughout the chapter. For example, what is the relationship between personality disorders and demon possession? How can one tell the difference between the two? Questions like these are important but, I regret, not the focus of this book. My purpose in raising these questions here is so that readers understand I am only dealing with one aspect of a complex subject. See the bibliography for further reading on deliverance.
2. Alan R. Tippett, *People Movements in Southern Polynesia* (Chicago: Moody, 1971).
3. C. Peter Wagner, "Special Kinds of Church Growth" (Class notes, Fuller Theological Seminary, 1984), 14.
4. Tippett, *People Movements*, 81.
5. Oscar Cullman, *Christ and Time* (Philadelphia: Westminster, 1964), 64.
6. Karl Ludwig Schmidt, "*Ethnos* in the NT," *Theological Dictionary of the New Testament*, vol. 2 (Grand Rapids, MI: Eerdmans, 1964), 369.
7. See Appendices A and B, where I give illustrations of power encounters in the history of the church.

8. John Wesley, *The Works of John Wesley*, 3rd ed. (Peabody, MA: Hendrickson Publishers, 1984) I:170.
9. Here is an example of the way people have responded to this kind of experience. Kevin Springer, after speaking at Emmaus Fellowship, a church in Ann Arbor, Michigan, in November of 1984, several months later received this letter from Martha Slauter, a woman he prayed for that day:

> I wanted to share with you my experiences since you prayed over me at Emmaus. I had asked you to pray for a spirit of bitterness and resentment to leave. You did that and then stopped and said you felt there was something more—and then said you thought I had a very hard time trusting people. You prayed over me for an anointing of God's own trust for people. I want to share with you that even after church I just *felt* trusting and felt the Lord doing something different in my relationships with the sisters. I felt the Lord ministering the love he has for me through them.
> When we came home from church and were discussing everything, I shared with Gary [her husband] that I wanted to go and talk with Dr. Dave King (a Christian counselor). That was significant in itself in that I never would have been open to that at all before. I've been under bondage to mistrust and letting circumstances get the best of me, to the point of sinking into self-pity and letting depression set in. The Lord showed me that he wanted to get these things taken care of once and for all, that he had victory for me and wanted to heal all these areas in me to enable me to go on with him, free of all encumbrances.
> Dr. King has been a blessing to both of us and has helped us uncover a lot of garbage. It has been like turning a light on—the searching light of God's Spirit. The Lord has really used the counseling to reveal some bad patterns in relating with people that I had developed just from the way I had been raised and through subsequent relationships before and after I came to the Lord. It has been incredible!
> The amazing thing to me is just how gentle and loving and merciful God's "spiritual surgery" is! The Lord also used two times I was prayed over and literally fell to the floor to do a lot of his work. I have never felt condemned by God as he points out all these problem areas, only tremendously reassured of his love and pleasure in me. I have previously had a problem in feeling condemned by everything.

10. Anonymous, "Where the Spirit of the Lord Is," *New Covenant* (October 1978): 15–16.
11. Werner Foerster, "*Exousia*," *Theological Dictionary of the New Testament*, vol. 2 (Grand Rapids, MI: Eerdmans, 1964), 568.

CHAPTER 3

1. I do not mean to imply that power evangelism is the only kind of evangelism practiced in the New Testament. Nor do I imply that power evangelism has been the most common type practiced by Christians throughout

church history. For example, evangelicals assert that the proclamation of the gospel message has intrinsic spiritual power, an assertion I would not deny. But my point remains: power evangelism was one of the normal kinds of evangelism in the early church and has surfaced throughout the history of the church with remarkable results.

2. The Gallup Poll (1983) and *The Yearbook of American and Canadian Churches* (1967 to 1983).
3. Joseph Bayly, "Keeping In Step: How Far Will American Evangelicals Follow Secular Cultural Trends?" *Pastoral Renewal* (October 1984): 34.
4. The National Opinion Research Center (affiliated with the University of Chicago) General Social Survey for 1983.
5. C. Peter Wagner, "A Third Wave?" *Pastoral Renewal* (July–August 1983): 1–5.
6. This statistic, an estimate, comes from many conversations with leading missiologists at Fuller Theological Seminary's School of World Mission. Cf. Craig Hanscome, "Predicting Missionary Dropout," *Evangelical Missions Quarterly* (1979): 152–55.
7. D. Martyn Lloyd-Jones, *Joy Unspeakable* (Eastbourne: Kingsway, 1984): 75.
8. C. S. Lewis, *Mere Christianity* (New York: MacMillan, 1943), 96.

CHAPTER 4

1. Viggo Sogaard, M.A. project, "Commissioned to Communicate: Cassettes in the Context of a Total Christian Communication Program," Wheaton Graduate School, Wheaton, Illinois. 1973. Also, cf. Viggo Sogaard, *Everything You Need to Know for a Cassette Ministry* (Minneapolis, MN: Bethany Publishing Company, 1975).
2. James Engel and Wilbert Norton, *What's Gone Wrong with the Harvest?* (Grand Rapids, MI: Zondervan, 1975), 45.

CHAPTER 5

1. James Sire, *The Universe Next Door* (Downers Grove, IL: InterVarsity Press, 1976), 17.
2. Charles Kraft, *Christianity and Culture* (Maryknoll, NY: Orbis Books, 1979).
3. Ibid., 53.
4. Ibid.
5. Harry Blamires, *The Christian Mind* (Ann Arbor, MI: Servant Books, 1978), 44.
6. Ibid.
7. Ibid., 67.
8. Ibid., 86.
9. Ibid., 106.
10. Jack Rogers, *Confessions of a Conservative Evangelical* (Philadelphia: Westminster, 1974), 33–34.
11. Paul Hiebert, "The Flaw of the Excluded Middle," *Missiology: An International Review*, vol. 10, no. 1 (January 1982): 35–47.
12. Kraft, *Christianity and Culture*, 60. Dr. Kraft shows how this assumption/

conclusion process works. Here are some cultural features and the assumptions and conclusions that are reached using each one:

CULTURAL FEATURE	ASSUMPTION	CONCLUSION
Clothing	1. Immodest to go naked (U.S.A.)	1. Must wear clothes even to bed.
	2. One covers one's body if hiding something (Gava people, Nigeria)	2. Go naked to prove yourself.
	3. For ornamentation only (Higi people, Nigeria)	3. Wear on occasion only. Rearrange or change in public.
Buying	1. Impersonal, economic transaction (U.S.A.)	1. Fixed prices. No interest in seller as person. Get it over quickly.
	2. Social, person-to-person affair (Africa, Asia, Latin America)	2. Dicker over price. Establish personal relationship. Take time.
Youthfulness	1. Desirable (U.S.A.)	1. Look young, act young. Use cosmetics.
	2. Tolerated; something to be overcome (Africa)	2. Prove yourself mature. Don't act young.
Age	1. Undesirable (U.S.A.)	1. Dreaded. Old people unwanted.
	2. Desirable (Africa)	2. Old people revered.
Education	1. Primarily formal, outside home, teacher-centered (U.S.A.)	1. Formal schools. Hired specialists.
	2. Primarily informal, in the home, learner-centered, traditional (Africa)	2. Learn by doing. Discipleship. Proverbs and folktales.

CHAPTER 6

1. Herman Ridderbos, *The Coming of the Kingdom* (Philadelphia: Presbyterian and Reformed, 1962), xi.
2. C. Peter Wagner, *Church Growth and the Whole Gospel* (New York: Harper

& Row, 1981). See also Luke 4:18–19; 7:21–22; Mark 16:17–18. (Note that I have added calming storms and feeding thousands.)

3. Ibid.

4. Rev. 21:1; cf. Colin Brown, *The International Dictionary of New Testament Theology,* vol. 2 (Grand Rapids, MI: Zondervan, 1976), 631.

5. *Evangelicals and Social Concern, An Evangelical Commitment,* No. 21, Grand Rapids Report, 1982, 9–11, 30–32.

6. James Dunn, *Jesus and the Spirit* (Philadelphia: Westminster, 1975), 48–49.

7. John Wilkinson, *Health and Healings* (New York: Columbia University Press, 1980). Wilkinson's analysis demonstrates that of all the verses in the Gospels, those related to healing are in the following proportions: Matthew, nine percent; Mark, twenty percent; Luke, twelve percent; John, thirteen percent.

8. Edward Langton, *Essentials of Demonology: A Study of Jewish and Christian Doctrine, Its Origin and Development* (London: Epworth Press, 1949), 173.

9. Jairus's daughter: Matthew 9:18–26; Mark 5:21–43; Luke 8:40–56. Lazarus: John 11:1–12:19. The widow's son: Luke 7:11–17; "holy people" at the crucifixion: Matthew 27:52. (Old Testament cases include: the widow of Zarephath's son, 1 Kings 17:17–24; the Shunammite woman's son, 2 Kings 4:18–37; Elisha's bones, 2 Kings 13:14–21. Other New Testament cases include: the "many holy people," Matthew 27:52–53; Peter raising Dorcas, Acts 9:36–42; Paul raising Eutychus, Acts 20:7–12.)

CHAPTER 7

1. Robert K. Johnston, ed. *The Use of the Bible in Theology—Evangelical Options* (Atlanta, GA: John Knox, 1985).

2. Signs and wonders:

Example	Result
By disciples (Acts 2:43)	Daily adding to church (2:47)
Power of God shown in mighty works (4:33)	Generosity among believers (4:34–35)
By Philip (8:6)	Samaria Church (8:12)
Hand of Lord with them (11:20–21; 13:11)	Great number believed and turned to the Lord (11:21)
Barnabas full of Spirit (11:24)	Great number brought to the Lord (11:24)
By Paul and Barnabas (14:1–7)	Believers (14:4)
Extraordinary miracles by Paul (19:11)	All churches in book of Revelation started during these two years

3. Speaking gifts:

Example	*Result*
Tongues (Acts 10:44)	Baptized believers (10:47)
Prophecy (13:1)	
Tongues/Prophecy (19:1–7)	Conversion of John the Baptist's disciples (19:5–7)

4. Visions:

Example	*Result*
Paul, Macedonian (Acts 16:8)	European churches
Paul (18:9)	Church at Corinth

5. Miracles:

Example	*Result*
Ananias/Sapphira (5:1–11)	Fear (5:13)
Spirit caught up Philip (8:39)	
Paul blinded (9:1–9a)	
Elymas blinded (13:4–12)	Sergius Paulus believed (13:12)
Paul stoned/raised (14:19–20)	Disciples (14:21)

6. Healings:

Example	*Result*
Lame man (3:7, 8)	Number grew to five thousand (4:4)
Sick and those tormented by evil spirits (5:16)	More healed (5:16)
Paul's blindness healed (9:17–19)	
Lame man in Lystra (14:10)	Disciples (14:21)
Demon expelled (16:18)	Brethren (16:40)
Publius's father's fever and dysentery (28:8)	All sick on island healed (28:9); church started according to church historians

7. Angelic visitation:

Example
Peter (12:7)
Paul (27:23, 24)

8.

Signs and Wonders	*Preaching*	*Church Growth*
2:4	2:14	2:41
3:1	3:12	4:4
8:6	8:6	8:12
8:26	8:35	8:38
10:3, 12, 44	10:34	10:47
11:20–21	11:20	11:21
11:23, 24	11:23	11:24b
13:1–3		Churches in Asia, Europe
14:1–7	14:3	14:4, 21, 22
14:8–18	14:15	14:21
16:16	16:14	16:40
16:25, 26	16:31	16:34
18:1	18:5	18:8
19:11	19:10	Churches in Asia

9. J. Sidlow Baxter, *Divine Healing of the Body* (Grand Rapids, MI: Zondervan, 1979), 52–65.

CHAPTER 8

1. C. Peter Wagner, "A Third Wave?" *Pastoral Renewal* (July–August 1983): 1–5.
2. Ibid., 4.
3. Richard Ostling, "Counting Every Soul on Earth," *Time* (May 3, 1982): 66–67.
4. Constance Jacquet, *Yearbook of American and Canadian Churches* (Nashville, TN: Abington, 1983), 225.
5. Ibid., 226.
6. Elmer Towns, "The World's Ten Largest Churches," *Christian Life* (January 1983): 60–66.
7. Victor Monterosso, William Reed, and Harman Johnson, *Latin American Church Growth* (Grand Rapids, MI: Eerdmans, 1969), 58.
8. C. Peter Wagner, *What Are We Missing?* (Carol Stream, IL: Creation House, 1973), 25.
9. C. Peter Wagner, *Your Spiritual Gifts Can Help Your Church Grow* (Ventura, CA: Regal, 1976), 32.
10. Vinson Synan, *In the Latter Days* (Ann Arbor, MI: Servant Books, 1984), 74.
11. Ibid., 74–75.
12. Vinson Synan, *The Holiness-Pentecostal Movement in the United States* (Grand Rapids, MI: Eerdmans, 1972), 144.
13. Synan, *In the Latter Days*, 79.
14. Ibid., 80.
15. Ibid., 81.
16. David Barrett, *World Christian Encyclopedia* (New York, Oxford University Press, 1982), 1–104.
17. Richard Quebedeaux, *The Young Evangelicals* (New York: Harper & Row, 1974), 42.
18. Dean Hoge, *Converts, Dropouts, and Returnees* (Washington, DC: United States Catholic Conference, 1981).
19. Michael Cassidy, *Bursting the Wineskins* (Wheaton, IL: Harold Shaw, 1983), 19; see also James Davison Hunter, *American Evangelicalism* (New Brunswick, NJ: Rutgers University Press, 1983), 7.
20. Ibid., 9; see also Quebedeaux, *The Young Evangelicals*, 13, 28–41.
21. John MacArthur, *The Charismatics* (Grand Rapids, MI: Zondervan, 1978), 131.
22. F. F. Bruce, *1 & 2 Corinthians* (London: Marshall, Morgan and Scott, 1971), 122.
23. Hunter, *American Evangelicalism*, 41–48.
24. Wagner, "A Third Wave?" 4–5.

CHAPTER 9

1. Andrew Murray, *The Believer's Full Blessing of Pentecost* (Minneapolis, MN: Bethany House, 1984), 9, 10.
2. A. W. Tozer, *How to Be Filled with the Holy Spirit* (Harrisburg, PA: Christian Publications, n.d.), 28.
3. "A gradual work of grace," Wesley wrote, "constantly precedes the instantaneous work both of justification and sanctification, but the work itself is undoubtedly instantaneous. . . . After a gradually increasing conviction of inbred sin you will be sanctified in a moment" (Letter of June 21, 1784, in *The Letters of Rev. John Wesley*, ed. John Telford. London: Epworth, 1931, 221–22.)
4. Vinson Synan, *In the Latter Days* (Ann Arbor, MI: Servant Books, 1984), 36–37. Cf. Frederick Dale Bruner, *A Theology of the Holy Spirit* (Grand Rapids, MI: Eerdmans, 1970), 37–39, 46–47.
5. D. Martyn Lloyd-Jones, *Joy Unspeakable* (Eastbourne: Kingsway, 1984), 80.
6. Reuben A. Torrey, *The Person and Work of the Holy Spirit* (New York: Revell, 1910), 176–210.
7. Reuben A. Torrey, *Baptism in the Holy Ghost* (London: James Nisbet, 1895), 16.
8. Synan, *Latter Days*, 45.
9. See Edward O'Connor, "Hidden Roots of the Charismatic Renewal in the Catholic Church," in Vinson Synan, *Aspects of Pentecostal-Charismatic Origins* (Plainfield, NJ: Logos International, 1975), 169–92.
10. Russell P. Spittler, "The Pentecostal Tradition: Reflections of an 'Ichthus'-iast, Part II," *Agora* (Fall 1977), 16.
11. The practice of baptizing new converts was (probably) introduced to the Jews by the Hillelites in the late intertestamental period. The Hillelites based the practice on Numbers 15:14 and Exodus 24:8. See Oscar Cullmann, *Baptism in the New Testament* (London: SCM, 1950), 11, 25.
12. Charles E. Hummel, *Fire in the Fireplace: Contemporary Charismatic Renewal* (Downers Grove, IL: InterVarsity Press, 1978), 185.
13. Russell Spittler, ed., *Perspectives on the New Pentecostalism* (Grand Rapids, MI: Baker, 1976), 186.
14. Spittler, "The Pentecostal Tradition, Part IV," *Agora* (Spring 1977), 11.
15. Ibid.
16. I will not discuss here the theories about the cessation of gifts like tongues. See my comments in Chapters 6 and 8.
17. Spittler, "The Pentecostal Tradition," 4.
18. Ibid., 6.
19. Another example of this new openness is found at the school of World Mission and Evangelism, Trinity Evangelical Divinity School (Evangelical Free Church of America) in Deerfield, Illinois. In the fall of 1985, Timothy M. Warner (former president of the Missionary denomination) taught a course entitled "ME 875M, Power Encounters in Missionary Ministry" in which course objectives were listed as follows:

    1. To explore the biblical concepts of spiritual power as they relate to God, Christ, the Holy Spirit, and angels and also to Satan and demons.

2. To understand the impact of worldviews which include the presence of absence of such concepts of power.

3. To identify and learn to cope with warfare between these powers as it affects the personal life of the Christian.

4. To acquire basic knowledge of how to minister to persons with problems related to demonic activity.

5. To identify and learn to cope with the places in ministry where the encounter between Christ's power and authority and demonic power is involved.

"ME 875M" was expected to attract about 25 students—a respectable enrollment for an elective course among the 1,200 member student body. Much to the divinity school's surprise, 81 students enrolled—a number large enough to make it one of the school's largest nonrequired courses.

At the same time, Kenneth S. Kantzer—Trinity Evangelical Divinity School's president and senior editor of *Christianity Today* magazine—taught a course on the history of the charismatic movement. This course, too, has attracted a large number of evangelical students.

20. C. S. Lewis, *Mere Christianity* (New York: MacMillan, 1943), 89.

APPENDIX B

1. Christiaan DeWet, "Signs and Wonders in Church Growth" (Masters thesis, School of World Mission, Fuller Theological Seminary, December 1981), 93–123.

2. Ibid., 95–96, 98 (note 3).

3. Ibid., 96–97.

4. Donald O. Young, "Signs and Wonders and Church Growth in the Ivory Coast" (Paper written for MC:510, "Signs, Wonders, and Church Growth," Fuller Theological Seminary, 1982).

5. Donald McGavran, "Healing and Evangelization of the World" (Syllabus, Basilia Church Growth Seminar, 1979), 296.

6. DeWet, "Signs and Wonders," 102, 106; cf. "But What About Hicks?" *Christian Century* (July 7, 1954): 814–815.

7. Donald McGavran, "Divine Healing and Church Growth," (Address delivered to a gathering of Christian and Missionary Alliance missionaries, Lincoln, Nebraska, 1979).

8. R. R. Cunville, "The Evangelization of Northeast India," (D.Miss. thesis, School of World Mission, Fuller Seminary, 1975), 156–79.

9. G. Elford, "Signs and Wonders Among the Canadian Indians," (Paper written for MC:510, "Signs, Wonders, and Church Growth," Fuller Theological Seminary, 1983).

Bibliography

Baird, Henry. *The Huguenots*. Vols. 1–2. New York: Scribner, 1895.

Baring-Gould, S. *The Lives of the Saints*. Vol. 3. London: John Nimmo, 1897.

Barker, Glenn, William Lane, and J. Ramsey Michaels. *The New Testament Speaks*. New York: Harper & Row, 1969.

Barratt, Thomas Ball. *When the Fire Fell*. Oslo, Norway: Hansen and Soner, 1927.

Barrett, David. *World Christian Encyclopedia*. New York: Oxford University Press, 1982.

Bartleman, Frank. *Azusa Street*. Plainfield, NJ: Logos, 1980.

Baxter, J. Sidlow. *Divine Healing of the Body*. Grand Rapids, MI: Zondervan, 1979.

Bennett, Dennis. *Nine O'Clock in the Morning*. Plainfield, NJ: Logos, 1970.

Blamires, Harry. *The Christian Mind*. Ann Arbor, MI: Servant Books, 1978.

———. *Where Do We Stand?* Ann Arbor, MI: Servant Books, 1980.

Bosworth, F. F. *Christ the Healer*. Old Tappan, NJ: Revell, 1973.

Bresson, Bernard L. *Studies in Ecstasy*. New York: Vantage Press, 1966.

Brumback, Carl. *Suddenly from People*. Springfield, MO: Gospel Publishing House, 1961.

Bruner, Frederick Dale. *A Theology of the Holy Spirit: The Pentecostal Experience and the New Testament*. Grand Rapids, MI: Eerdmans, 1970.

Cassidy, Michael. *Bursting the Wineskins*. Wheaton, IL: Harold Shaw, 1983.

The Catholic Encyclopedia Dictionary. New York: The Gilmary Society, 1941.

Cho, Paul Yonggi. *The Fourth Dimension*. Plainfield, NJ: Logos International, 1979.

Christenson, Larry. *A Message to the Charismatic Movement*. Weymouth, MA: Dimension, 1972.

Coxe, A. Cleveland. *The Ante-Nicene Fathers.* Vols. 1, 3–6. Grand Rapids, MI: Eerdmans, 1951.

Cross, Whitney R. *The Burned-over District.* New York: Harper & Row, 1950.

Cullman, Oscar. *Christ and Time.* Philadelphia: Westminster, 1964.

Defferari, Joseph, ed. *The Fathers of the Church.* Vol. 9, St. Basil, *Ancetial Works.* Vol. 15, *Early Christian Biographies.* Vol. 24, St. Augustine, *City of God. Books 17–22.* Vol. 25, St. Hilary of Poitiers, *The Trinity.* Vol. 39, St. Gregory The Great, *Dialogues.* Vol. 44, St. Ambrose, *Theological and Dogmatic Works.* Vol. 58, St. Gregory of Nyssa, *Ascetical Works.* Washington, DC: The Catholic University of America Press, 1947.

Dix, Gregory, ed. *The Treatise of the Apostolic Tradition.* London: SPCK, 1968.

Douglas, J. D., ed. *The New International Dictionary of the Christian Church.* Grand Rapids, MI: Zondervan, 1974.

Drummond, Andrew L. *Edward Irving and His Circle.* London: James Clark, n.d.

Dudden, F. Homes. *Gregory the Great.* New York: Russell & Russell, 1905.

Dunn, James D. G. *Baptism in the Holy Spirit.* Napierville, IL: Allenson, 1970.

———. *Jesus and The Spirit.* Philadelphia: Westminster, 1975.

Easton, Burton, ed. *The Apostolic Tradition of Hippolytos.* Cambridge: Cambridge University Press, 1934.

Elliot, Elisabeth. *The Savage My Kinsman.* Ann Arbor, MI: Servant Books, 1981.

Fordsham, Stanley. *Smith Wigglesworth: Apostle of Faith.* Springfield, MO: Radiant Books, 1948.

Fox, George. *The Journal of George Fox.* 2 vols. London: Friends Tract Association, 1901.

Frazier, Claude, ed. *Faith Healing: Finger of God? or Scientific Curiosity?* New York: Thomas Nelson, 1973.

Gibbs, Eddie. *I Believe in Church Growth.* London: Hodder & Stoughton, 1981.

Giles, John A., ed. *The Venerable Bede's Ecclesiastical History of England,* 2nd ed. (New York: AMS Press, 1971).

Gordon, A. J. *The Ministry of Healing.* Harrisburg, PA: Christian Publication, 1802.

Grant, Robert. *Ignatius of Antioch.* Vol. 4 of *The Apostolic Fathers.* London: Thomas Nelson, 1966.

Grant, Robert M. *Augustine to Constantine*. New York: Harper & Row, n.d.

———. *Second Century Christianity*. London: SPCK, 1946.

Green, Michael. *I Believe in the Holy Spirit*. London: Hodder & Stoughton, 1975.

Grossman, Siegfried. *Charisma: The Gifts of the Spirit*. Wheaton, IL: Key Publications, 1971.

Harper, Michael. *As at the Beginning: The Twentieth Century Pentecostal Revival*. London: Hodder & Stoughton, 1965.

———. *Three Sisters*. Wheaton, IL: Tyndale House, 1979.

Harrell, David Allen. *All Things Are Possible*. Bloomington, IN: Indiana University Press, 1975.

Hermann, Placid, ed. *St. Francis of Assisi*. Chicago: Herald Press, n.d.

Hummel, Charles E. *Fire in the Fireplace*. Downers Grove, IL: InterVarsity Press, 1978.

Hunter, A. M. *Christ and the Kingdom*. Edinburgh: The Saint Andrew Press, 1980.

Hunter, James Davison. *American Evangelicalism*. New Brunswick, NJ: Rutgers University Press, 1983.

Jacquet, Constance. *Yearbook of American and Canadian Churches*. Nashville, TN: Abington, 1983.

Johnston, Robert K., ed. *The Use of the Bible in Theology—Evangelical Options*. Atlanta, GA: John Knox, 1985.

Kallas, James. *The Satanward View: A Study in Pauline Theology*. Philadelphia: Westminster, 1966.

———. *Jesus and The Power of Satan*. Philadelphia: Westminster, 1968.

———. *The Real Satan*. Minneapolis, MN: Augsburg, 1975.

Kavanaugh, Kienan, ed. *The Collected Works of St. Teresa of Avila*. Washington, DC: ICS Publications, 1976.

Kelsey, Morton T. *Tongue Speaking: An Experiment in Spirit Experience*. New York: Doubleday, 1964.

———. *Tongues Speaking*. London: Hodder & Stoughton, 1968.

———. *Healing and Christianity*. New York: Harper & Row, 1976.

Kraft, Charles H. *Christianity and Culture*. Maryknoll, NY: Orbis Books, 1979.

Kraft, Robert. *Barnabas and the Didache*. Vol. 3 of *The Apostolic Fathers*. London: Thomas Nelson, 1965.

Kreiser, Robert. *Miracles, Convulsions, and Ecclesiastical Politics in Early Eighteenth-Century Paris*. Princeton, NJ: Princeton University Press, 1978.

Ladd, George Eldon. *Jesus and the Kingdom*. New York: Harper & Row, 1964.

————. *A Theology of the New Testament.* Grand Rapids, MI: Eerdmar.ɔ. 1974.

Langton, Edward. *Essentials of Demonology: A Study of Jewish and Christian Doctrine, Its Origin and Development.* London: 1949.

Lasch, Christopher. *Haven in a Heartless World.* New York: Basic Books, 1977.

Laurentin, Rene. *Catholic Pentecostalism.* Garden City, NY: Image Books, 1978.

Lindsell, Harold. *The Holy Spirit in the Latter Days.* Nashville, TN: Thomas Nelson, 1983.

Lloyd-Jones, D. Martyn. *Joy Unspeakable.* Eastbourne: Kingsway Publications, 1984.

Martin, Ralph. *Fire on the Earth.* Ann Arbor, MI: Servant Books, 1975.

MacArthur, John. *The Charismatics.* Grand Rapids, MI: Zondervan, 1978.

MacNutt, Francis. *Healing.* Notre Dame, IN: Ave Maria Press, 1974.

McDonald, William G., gen. ed. *New Catholic Encyclopedia.* Vol. 14. Washington, DC: The Catholic University of America, 1967.

McDonnell, Kilian, and Arnold Bittlinger. *The Baptism of the Holy Spirit as an Ecumenical Problem.* South Bend, IN: Charismatic Renewal Services, 1972.

Monden, Louis. *Signs and Wonders.* New York: Desclee, 1960.

Moore, Louis. *The Visitor.* N.p., n.d.

Murray, Andrew. *The Believer's Full Blessing of Pentecost.* Minneapolis, MN: Bethany House, 1984.

Nickalls, John, ed. *The Journal of George Fox.* London: Religious Society of Friends, 1975.

Olsson, Karl A. *By One Spirit.* Chicago: Covenant Press, 1962.

Oswald, Hilton, ed. *Luther's Works.* Vol. 25. Saint Louis, MO: Concordia, n.d.

Packer, James I. *Keep in Step with the Spirit.* Old Tappan, NJ: Revell, 1984.

Parker, Percy Livingstone, ed. *The Journal of John Wesley.* Chicago: Moody, n.d.

Penn-Lewis, Jessie. *The Awakening in Wales.* Ft. Washington, PA: Christian Literature Crusade, n.d.

Pilkington, J. G., ed. *The Confessions of St. Augustine.* New York: Liveright, 1963.

Price, Charles S. *And Signs Followed.* Plainfield, NJ: Logos, 1972.

Quebedeaux, Richard. *The Young Evangelicals.* New York: Harper & Row, 1974.

————. *The New Charismatics.* New York: Doubleday, 1976.

————. *The Worldly Evangelicals*. New York: Harper & Row, 1978.

————. *The New Charismatics II: How a Christian Renewal Movement Became Part of the American Religious Mainstream*. San Francisco: Harper & Row, 1983.

Rahner, Karl. *Spiritual Exercises*. London: Herder and Herder, 1962.

Ranaghan, Kevin, and Dorothy Ranaghan. *Catholic Pentecostals*. Paramus, NJ: Paulist Press, 1969.

Sandford, John, and Paula Sandford. *The Transformation of the Inner Man*. South Plainfield, NJ: Bridge, 1982.

Schaff, Philip, and Henry Wace. *Nicene and Post-Nicene Fathers*. Series 1: Vols. 1, 7, 8, 12, 16. Series 2: Vols. 1, 6, 7. Grand Rapids, MI: Eerdmans, n.d.

Sire, James. *The Universe Next Door*. Downers Grove, IL: InterVarsity Press, 1976.

————. *Scripture Twisting*. Downers Grove, IL: InterVarsity Press, 1980.

Snyder, Graydon, F. *Hermas*. Vol. 6 of *The Apostolic Fathers*. London: Thomas Nelson, n.d.

Spittler, Russell P., ed. *Perspectives on the New Pentecostalism*. Grand Rapids, MI: Baker, 1976.

Synan, Vinson. *The Holiness-Pentecostal Movement in the United States*. Grand Rapids, MI: Eerdmans, 1972.

————. *Charismatic Bridges*. Ann Arbor, MI: Word of Life, 1974.

————. *In the Latter Days*. Ann Arbor, MI: Servant Books, 1984.

Tappert, Theodore B., ed. *Luther: Letters of Spiritual Counsel*. Vol. 18 of the Library of Christian Classics. Philadelphia: Westminster, n.d.

Telford, John, ed. *The Letters of John Wesley*. Vol. 2. London: Epworth, n.d.

Thompson, A. H., ed. *Bede, His Life, Times and Writings*. London: Oxford University Press, n.d.

Tippett, Alan R. *People Movements in Southern Polynesia*. Chicago: Moody, 1971.

Tydings, Judith. *Gathering a People*. N.p., n.d.

Vine, W. E. *An Expository Dictionary of New Testament Words*. Westwood, NJ: Revell, 1940.

Vos, Geerhardus. *The Kingdom of God and the Church*. Nutley, NJ: Presbyterian and Reformed Publishing, 1972.

Wagner, C. Peter. *Frontiers in Missionary Strategy*. Chicago: Moody, 1972.

————. *What Are We Missing?*. (Formerly titled *Look Out! the Pentecostals Are Coming*). Carol Stream, IL: Creation House, 1973.

————. *Your Church Can Grow*. Ventura, CA: Regal, 1976.

————. *Your Spiritual Gifts Can Help Your Church Grow*. Ventura, CA: Regal, 1976.

————. *Church Growth and the Whole Gospel*. New York: Harper & Row, 1981.

————. *On the Crest of the Wave*. Ventura, CA: Regal, 1983.

Warfield, Benjamin B. *Counterfeit Miracles*. Carlisle, PA: The Banner of Truth Trust, 1918.

Warren, Max. *I Believe in the Great Commission*. London: Hodder & Stoughton, 1976.

Watson, David. *I Believe in Evangelism*. London: Hodder & Stoughton, 1976.

————. *Called & Committed*. London: Hodder & Stoughton, 1981.

Wells, David. *Revolution in Rome*. Downers Grove, IL: InterVarsity Press, 1972.

Woodworth-Etter, Maria. *Her Life and Ministry*. Dallas, TX: Christ for the Nation, 1976.